Strategic Engagement

Strategic Engagement

*Practical Tools to Raise Morale
and Increase Results*

Volume I: Core Activities

Chris Crosby

Edited by Gary Gesell

BUSINESS EXPERT PRESS

Strategic Engagement: Practical Tools to Raise Morale and Increase Results
Volume I: Core Activities
Copyright © Business Expert Press, LLC, 2019.

First published in 2019 by
Business Expert Press, LLC
222 East 46th Street, New York, NY 10017
www.businessexpertpress.com

ISBN-13: 978-1-63157-662-1 (print)
ISBN-13: 978-1-63157-663-8 (e-book)

Business Expert Press Strategic Management Collection

Collection ISSN: 1946-5637 (print)
Collection ISSN: 1946-5645 (electronic)

Cover and interior design by S4Carlisle Publishing Services Private Ltd., Chennai, India
Graphics created by Chris Crosby with special contributions from Celeste Crosby

First edition: 2019

10 9 8 7 6 5 4 3 2 1

Printed in the United States of America

To John, Robert, Gilmore, Merlyn, Celeste, and Gary.
Thank you for your love and support!

～

Special thanks to Ronald Lippitt, Richard Walton, Kurt
Lewin, John Wallen, and Richard Schmuck. Without your
foundational work, Robert P Crosby may not have had
the tools to synthesize this rich collection of activities.

～

Tremendous gratitude to Robert P Crosby: my father,
trainer, and mentor throughout my career. These volumes
highlight his ability to design and deliver strategic
activities to solve problems. They provide a definitive
list of his designs, which generated unheard-of business
results, the core second-year curriculum of his unique
corporate graduate program, and more.

Abstract

Volume I of *Strategic Engagement* covers four core activities from my unique graduate experience under the tutelage of Robert P Crosby. The activities include two forms of third-party conflict (boss–employee and employee–employee), transition meetings, and work team development.

Robert P Crosby is a unique figure in Organization Development (OD). Despite only needing a few more credits, he bypassed a doctorate (had no plans to teach) to pursue his drive to apply learnings in group dynamics to various settings. Ironically, while continually "applying" at all levels of organizations and being mentored for three decades by Dr. Ronald Lippitt, he created and taught a graduate program for a quarter century.

OD significantly expanded after World War II, with the first T-Group experience in 1947. Crosby, whose first T-Group was in 1953, is an integrator who solves client problems rather than impose any one theory. His corporate graduate program within Alcoa included managers and hourlies (often unionized) who were expected to implement their learnings after each module to create better results and higher morale.

Kurt Lewin, the T-Group creator, fled Hitler and studied how authority is manifested in leaders. Lewin is called "the practical theorist." These weeklong T-Group modules were created to ensure immediate relevance to the workplace. Marvin Weisbord quoted Lewin in his foundational book *Productive Workplaces* (2012, 3rd Edition, p. 92): "'Autocracy is imposed on the individual,' he wrote (pp. 81-82). 'Democracy he has to learn!'. . . a core technology of leader development to this day."

Robert P Crosby's perspective on OD was highly influenced by his extensive work at the floor level. Through his unique experience and mentorships, he created a theory of authority in systems (see *Strategic Organizational Alignment*, Chapter 1: Authority).

Volume I and Volume II are filled with activities to create movement in your organizations to directly impact the bottom line while positively engaging your employees. Volume II focuses on system-wide activities and includes group-to-group conflict, goal alignment, process improvement, and project or major initiative.

Keywords

alignment; business results; change; change management; conflict; cross-functional; leadership; MBA; organization development; productivity; project; organizational development; project management; Stanford; survey feedback; team; transitions; workgroup; workplace

Advanced Quotes for *Strategic Engagement Practical Tools to Raise Morale and Increase Results Volume I: Core Activities*

"Chris Crosby has followed up his insightful first book, *Strategic Organizational Alignment: Authority, Power, Results*, with a well-written and well-organized sequel that expands upon the territory he illuminates in the aforementioned book and explores new and promising horizons. Crosby's two-volume book, ***Strategic Engagement,*** highlights eight practical core OD interventions that are needed today more than ever. This book is engaging, compelling, and replete with practical knowledge and wisdom."
—William L. Weis, PhD, Professor of Management, Albers School of Business and Economics, Seattle University

"Treehouse has benefitted from the pragmatic strategies presented in Strategic Engagement. Working directly with Chris Crosby while developing a team of facilitators capable of delivering many of these interventions in-house, Treehouse has gained alignment, reduced tension, and improved our plans for major initiatives. Facilitated conversations between individual employees, managers, and employees and groups within the organization have enhanced communication. As a non-profit, we are resource constrained and benefit from the efficiencies gained through this work. I highly recommend this book!"
—Janis Avery, CEO, Treehouse

"Chris has done a remarkable thing here. He has packaged the very tools he used to help me transform multiple workplaces in a way that is accessible and usable for all. These books are invaluable."
—Behzad Suroosh, Regional VP Supply Chain Americas, Beiersdorf AG

"If you really want to change and improve your company, then you must read this book! Chris lays out a strategy based on actual experiences that created demonstrable enhancements in a variety of environments, including my own companies."
—Clive Copsey, Global Director of New Product Development Alcoa

"Chris Crosby has provided us with a virtual outline for a graduate-level program in OD!
    Amazing work, Chris!"
— Dr. John J. Scherer, Director, Scherer Leadership International Co-Creator, the Original LIOS MA-ABS Program Author, *Wiser at Work: Five Questions that Change Everything*

"*Strategic Engagement* (Volumes 1 and 2) offers practical and powerful tools to address critical challenges facing teams and organizations. The books address several important focus areas, including Conflict, Goal Alignment, Process Improvement, Transition Meetings, and Work Group Development. Chris has done a fantastic job of making it simple, easy to understand, and implement. An important book for all OD practitioners and consultants, it will provide ready access to critical interventions applicable for teams and organizations."
—Ragland Thomas, Vice President—Global Organization Development & Strategy, Institute of Organization Development

"I have an extensive collection of business books, and this one is a real gem. I started my last two CEO positions with transition sessions as outlined in this collection and led by Chris himself. The activities in this book are the very activities I have used to lead to record results. I find it a remarkable collection and written in a way that is easy to comprehend and immediately effective."
—Brian Bauerbach, President & CEO, Mold Rite Plastics

"An immensely practical book packed with knowledge and wisdom to help people create efficient and effective organizations that get results. Chris has expertly synthesized and organized what can be an overwhelming amount of information and conceptual material into an easy-to-understand guide. Not only is this book tremendously helpful for professionals, managers and executives should read it with no less reverence than they would read their company's financial report."
—Ethan Schutz, President & CEO, The Schutz Company

"*Strategic Engagement* (Volumes 1 and 2) provides practitioners and leaders clear ways to improve productivity. The book blends theory with practice and allows organizations to create productive and engaged workplaces. Through step-by-step instruction, Crosby shows you how to navigate group-to-group conflict, articulate and align goals, and improve both processes and project initiatives. A must read for anyone in the field."
—Rodney D. Coates, Professor, Global and Intercultural Studies, Miami University of Ohio

"An exceptionally clear and comprehensive two-volume book with relevant in-depth theories, practical steps, and specific tools to accomplish your goals.
A 'must read' for every leader and consultant."
—Brenda Kerr Minno, President, the Leadership Institute of Seattle

"This book is a great 'pocket book'—it's a leader's best friend—saturated with a road map that puts theory into action.

An organization is a 'network of relationships'. Crosby takes this maxim seriously, highlighting the many ways this network of relationships can fumble while providing clear steps for upgrading the entire system. Too many books give glamour to theory while missing the link of how theory is implemented.

I believe his book offers a bonus—the practice associated with this book not only leads to better results, but will lead to greater joy within the 'network of relationships' in the workplace. What a great bonus for such a great book."

—Timothy Weber, PhD, Licensed Clinical Psychologist

"The chapter called software basics is the blueprint of our change management strategy when we implemented a division global ERP system. Our roll-out was a success due to that strategy led by Chris. Many companies can have a successful technical ERP solution, but without the end users and business leader aligned and fully informed of the benefits and risk you can't have a successful ERP roll-out. It took everyone on the team to make our ERP implementation a success, but Chris's work on educating the business leaders and making sure the process owner's voices were heard about benefits and risk elevated our implementation from good to excellent."

—Mark Howard, Hawaii Operational Manager, Serta/Simmons

Contents

Appendices

List of Figures

Preface

"The best theory is appreciative inquiry!"
"Which theory shall we use to drive our change?"
"The best way forward is a new form of collaboration!"
"Let's measure engagement and create trainings to increase it!"
"Feedback techniques are the answer to solving our goals!"
"We must use lean manufacturing on everything!"
"The best theory is dialogic OD!"

In a world obsessed with searching for the newest theory, this book provides a set of strategic activities that, if executed well, will result in higher productivity, improved morale, and measurable results.

The activities are by no means a comprehensive list of what you can do but represent the core of what was used in multiple locations that led to turnarounds of immense success and almost unheard-of productivity gains. Moreover, all metrics will move in a positive direction when combined with strong sponsorship and alignment throughout your organization, as discussed in my first book *Strategic Organizational Alignment (SOA)*.

These activities are the brainchild of Robert P Crosby. Through the course of his career, Robert P Crosby created ways to facilitate strategic engagement activities aimed at solving one-on-one, group, or cross-functional issues. He then used them to achieve results at all levels of organizations and as the foundation of his many successful culture change efforts. What follows are step-by-step guides to each activity. Learn how to facilitate them, as-is, or adapt them to your unique situation.

The activities may seem simple, yet they are profound in their ability to involve all the hearts and minds in your organization to achieve a common goal. That is the essence of engagement. And what is the goal? The goal is to create a thriving workplace that 1) *achieves its business metrics*, 2) *provides excellent service(s) or product(s) to its customers*, and 3) *develops and grows its employees*.

Why These Activities?

These activities are the core group taught to me and used in multiple, successful culture-change efforts. I have successfully used them throughout the world.

Are They All I Will Need?

Probably not, but that is up to each individual practitioner or business leader. These activities solve most of the problems in your organization while simultaneously strengthening work relationships. They are created with the belief that once you know your problems, you can solve them. Each activity provides a model aimed at a specific situation to gather issues, facilitate constructive dialogue, choose a course of action, track each action with clear accountability, and follow through until resolution. Plus, they create a climate of inclusion because they are aimed at all employees and do not allow any employee to stay passive in improving the workplace.

Yet, what may flush out, depending on your situation, are specific problems that need solving beyond the capabilities of any single employee. An expert method must be used. There are many types of methods intended to solve specific problems that require training and expertise in a particular practice such as Lean Manufacturing or Six Sigma. Those or any other practical problem-solving methods that an internal employee has can and should be used.

This book includes problem-solving methods intended to raise issues that are well within the skill sets of most employees. The methods solve problems that have remained chronic despite being quite solvable, yet the workplace has been unable to get organized and *aligned* to resolve. If you do not have the expertise for certain problem-solving methods, then you can obtain the talent through a new hire or a consultant.

The Importance of Mental Models

In a classic study, participants were placed in a group experience that included a variety of growth groups including encounter, gestalt, and T-Groups. Participants were followed during the next year to see how well they functioned in conflictual moments. Students that had a mental model around conflict were best able to cope through difficult situations. Further, it was discovered that it did not matter what mental model was used, only that they used a mental model.

Almost every book I reference provides a series of practical mental models to use when needed. The ability to function in tense moments is directly related to self-awareness and your ability to use a mental model. The activities in this book are grounded in ways of thinking that allow for an engaged culture to emerge.

Each chapter outlining a strategic engagement activity lists the core mental models. The following mental models inform my books.

- Openness vs. Personal Confession
- Sponsor/Agent/Target/Advocate (SATA)
- Decision Making
- Follow-up
- Accountability
- Structure
- The Interpersonal Gap
- SOCIAL STYLE
- SIPOC Model
- Waterline Model
- Victim/Creator ("I" Language)
- **Four Key Interpersonal Skills**: Behavioral Description, Feeling Description, Paraphrase, and Perception Check

There is a progression that helps one become more functional in tense moments. First, you must have *awareness*. Second, you must have a *mental model* to help navigate the experience. Third, you must have a set of core behavioral interpersonal *skills*. Finally, you must have the *discipline* to use the mental models and interact using the behavioral skills. Having and building the capacity to use such models adds sanity in moments that would otherwise give rise to reactivity and potential chaos.

Courage

Engagement cultures are built with *courage*. It is not about comfort. It is about *moving in* to difficult topics with grace while using specific behavioral interactive skills. Then, it is about hanging in and working through them so that when you *move out* you have issues clarified, solutions identified, and agreements made with clear accountability (Single Point Accountability, What, and By-When). Such cultures follow up until the new normal is in place and working. Avoiding issues, people, or difficult topics and cultures where blame is the norm is the opposite of an engagement culture. The mantra of engagement is "feel what you feel; choose what you do." That choice should be made with clarity of what is best for the organization and with your rising *courage* to work through difficult moments. When issues are solved with clear accountability, then real moments of *happiness*, *pride* of accomplishment, improved business results, and *fun* happen with greater frequency.

Openness vs. Personal Confession

Individuals and organizations must be open to ensure peak performance. Only with openness does data flow through organizations with the speed and clarity needed to cope with change. The concept of openness can sound threatening when people confuse *being open* with *personal confession*. A vital difference exists between these two concepts. The following distinction will help clarify the difference. Personal confession is the sharing of private, personal information about one's self and is often about past events. Openness describes what is happening now.

Feedback using openness is specific, clear, descriptive, and timely ("I liked the fact that you condensed your summary to one page"). In personal confession, people talk about their personal life. Conversation in a *personal confession* is from one's private, internal experience.

Openness deals with the immediate situation ("You're asking me for this report by Wednesday noon, but I do not think I can finish it by then"). Organizations need that type of openness. With *personal confession* norms predominating, such feedback is often withheld for fear of hurting feelings, being hurt, or being too personal. Such confusion between openness (which organizations need) and *personal confession* (which is appropriate with a counselor or differentiated friend) encourages closed behavior that negatively affects organizations.

The Challenge of Learning Openness

Openness is essential if data are to flow freely through organizations. Learning openness requires training in differentiation. Differentiation is a prerequisite skill not only to *resolve* but to *use* conflict well.

Openness is being specific, concrete, and nonjudgmental rather than general and judgmental. A person's primary commitment in an open organization is to "tell it like it is"—not in the old school sense of being judgmental and accusative but in the new sense of being specific and nonjudgmental and toward achieving the organization's mission. A true leader describes life's situations without blaming others. The goal is to *make it work* rather than *find fault or blame.*

Differentiated training goes beyond that which all but the boldest organizations care to endure today. But the willingness to assume such training will define those organizations that are the most productive while also being the most humane. We need people with skills that go beyond completing minimal work. We must equip a manager to become a mentor, teacher, and wise person, who by word, tone, and deed displays the heart and soul of an open, productive organization. This manager will balance management authority and employee influence.

This book delivers a series of activities and a platform for your employees to be more open. Each activity provides steps to turn interpretive data into specific, open data regarding the current state. If your employees cannot reach openness and instead continue fighting about judgments or interpretations, then they need a larger training to increase their emotional intelligence and interpersonal skill such as a T-Group that is adapted for industry.

Engagement

Engaged employees are excited about work. They contribute their ideas, participate in dialogue, focus on workplace improvement, and feel pride in their accomplishments. They are way beyond punching a time clock. Engaged workplaces are filled with such employees, and it becomes infectious. Even if you are not excited about work, an engaged workplace delivers structured meetings where you contribute ideas and participate in the conversation.

Engagement Is a Choice

All *leaders* and *managers* must understand that *whether or not their workplace is engaged is their choice.* The choice to be engaged is ironically not primarily the employees, but rather the employees' direct manager. Managers set expectations, create structures, and provide opportunities for employees to engage to achieve results within and outside their immediate work team.

This is not a passive role. If an employee is not engaging or actively disengaging, then you must appropriately intervene. Using your legitimate authority is critical to ensure the employees gain opportunities to improve the workplace. Once employees start contributing on a regular basis, even if they are shy or introverted, then engagement becomes contagious. Therefore, leaders must create opportunities and stay firm in moments when employees push against them. This allows creativity and passion within the workforce to emerge.

Most managers are not trained in how to create a structure that ensures engagement; they typically do the opposite. Everyone knows how to disengage if the boss says, "Any questions?" How many times does that lead to actual questions? Most likely it leads to a room of silent people staring at each other and hoping nobody says anything so they can leave.

This book will help you change those dynamics, at the right moments, to shift your culture to one of engagement. But not engagement only for engagement sake; *the purpose is to engage to get better business results*. A nice by-product of those results is that creating an engagement culture significantly improves your employees' morale and positively impacts all key metrics, including turnover, absenteeism, safety, quality, productivity, sales, and profitability.

Engagement Removes Barriers and Yields Results

Engagement helps your system heal. Carl Rogers summarized the basic hypothesis as follows:

> "If I can provide a certain type of relationship, the other person will discover within himself the capacity to use that relationship for growth and change, and personal development will occur" (Rogers, 1961, p. 33).

Applying this concept to organizations means that if you manage and create structures that support positive interaction, then your employees will engage and apply themselves to solve most, if not all, of the internal problems facing your workplace.

Fast-forward to the 2017 *Gallup State of the American Workplace Report* and Gallup confirms what Rogers' hypothesized. If your boss is actively engaged, then you have a 59% higher probability of being an engaged employee. Furthermore, companies that have the highest percentage of engaged employees have the best performance metrics across the board. The real question is not just one of engagement, but rather *how do you increase engagement between the boss and their direct reports?* That is the big payoff. Beyond that, how do you engage the right people at the right time to solve the right things?

Engagement Takes Persistence

If you think you can increase engagement by giving a theory or attempting to measure it, then think again. Engagement increases by applying the following core items.

1. Change the *structure* of *key events* in your organization to ensure effective interaction.
2. Structure how employees raise issues and *never shoot the messenger*.

3. Focus on *accountability at every level* of the organization (see Chapter 7 of *SOA*).

4. *Apply selected activities* in this book to ensure that all employees' voices are heard, even the most introverted, and use them on a consistent basis.

5. *Follow up* on each action created until it is in place and fixing the intended problems or a viable alternative is working.

6. *Balance authority* toward the middle of the authority continuum while allowing employees to take as much initiative as appropriate but never in an ideological way (see Chapters 12 and 13 of *SOA*).

7. *Stay persistent* because engagement for results is a journey with no end. Getting off the path is much easier than staying on it, yet being on the path yields amazing results.

Engagement takes time, strategy, and persistence. Set your course and do your best to stay on the path. Small turns on the path will not hurt your overall progress. *You must stay strong to truly create an engagement culture.* If you do so, the rewards will be immense.

Engagement Is Not a Free-for-all

Do not confuse engagement with a boundaryless culture where all employees can do whatever they want. I call that type of chaos anarchy, and it is toward the high permissive continuum of managing people. In fact, many managers who fear being too autocratic manage from this extreme yet do so in a passive way. To create a real engagement culture, leaders must take a stand to ensure employee participation.

Participation is not without boundaries. Issues must be captured and clarified no matter who raised them, regardless of what others may think.

The distinction here is that *all employees deserve to be heard, yet a clear decision process must be used to determine which issues will be addressed.* Each issue must be clarified so employees, including the manager, fully understand the issue. All workplaces have a finite amount of resources, so managers must choose what they can or cannot do given the current situation. This process is vital and must be known before making decisions so employees trust their manager.

It is impossible to satisfy all employees by working on all problems, yet most, if not all, will better respect decisions if they are aware of the decision-making process. *The trap that many make is to say no to even capturing employees' issues.* Consequently, managers are actively creating disgruntled or disengaged employees. Even exceptional employees stop volunteering when their ideas are not considered.

Effective engagement is not a free-for-all; it is quite the opposite. Effective engagement only happens when managers actively use their legitimate authority to create a healthy set of boundaries and structures that ensure dispersed participation and accountability for all.

How to Use These Volumes

The basic task of all organizations is to engage their people to achieve goals. This book delivers a set of activities specifically focused on how to do just that.

Since the Gallup Organization published their extensive study on engagement in the workplace, engagement has become one of the many buzzwords filling organizations. Gallup's findings were shocking but also predictable. Gallup found, in their 2013 study *The Global State of the Workplace Report*, that "Worldwide, Actively Disengaged Employees Outnumber Engaged Employees by Nearly 2 to 1." In 2017, Gallup published their state of the American Workplace Report and also found the numbers are dismal. Only 33% of workers are considered engaged, while 67% are not, and in that 67%, 15% are actively disengaged. Since 2013, engagement has become a buzzword, with many rushing to measure and teach trainings in the virtues of engagement. While most are well intentioned, the truth is that *engagement for engagement sake is a disaster.* To create an effective engagement culture, you must know how to engage the right people, at the right time, to solve the right things, all while using the right structure.

So how do you do it? The answer lies ahead . . .

Four Key Ingredients for Engagement and Results

1. **Align Sponsors to Clear Goals:** Clear goals are measurable, balanced, realistic, and achievable. In Chapter 2 of *SOA* (and Appendix E of this book), I discuss distinctions that must be met when identifying workplace goals. Measurable goals create healthy engagement in your workplace. Why? Because goals are to be used as a focusing and filtering devise for all employees.

   If your goals are just adjectives with no metrics, then it is nearly impossible to know whether you are achieving them or to use them to focus on the right issues. Lack of clarity about direction leads to power struggles about what to do and increases the odds that a "test of wills" between employees will determine actions. In contrast, clearly defined and understood numeric, measurable goals allow managers and their employees a filter when conflict happens over direction. Effective managers use such clarity to determine direction and make their best guess on how to achieve results.

Set numerically measurable goals based on your best marketing information to establish a clear direction. Be transparent about how you created your numbers and the potential costs of not achieving them. Then broaden your goals to include the work processes that must be improved to reach the bottom-line goals (BLG). Include your employees to ensure you focus on the right processes.

Use a structured dialogue to align your leaders to the goals. Alignment happens through dialogue. Therefore, if you typically e-mail your goals or allow employees outside the legitimate authority structure to build goals by department (such as employees creating a balanced scorecard or conducting strategic planning), then make sure to follow up with dialogue to approve each group's goals. Each leader must own and understand the goals they are working toward and then methodically involve their employees to achieve those goals (see Chapter 3, Goal Alignment, of Volume II).

2. **Identify the Right Employees:** Once your goals are clear, then determine the appropriate employees to achieve them. For a work team improvement activity referenced in Chapters 3 and 4 (or 2 of Volume II), the right employees are obvious. Yet, for any sort of process, project, or problem-solving improvement activity, it is critical to balance the people doing the work with technical experts and managers. Re-read Chapter 9 of *SOA* to ensure you properly involve all employees to achieve your goals. To transform your organization, you may need to intervene one workgroup at a time until you involve your entire workplace. The process of cascading is explained on p. 54 of Volume II or p. 205 of *SOA*. Reference the SATA chart in Chapter 6 of *SOA* for guidance on how to include appropriate employees to resolve specific issues.

3. **Use a Structured Activity:** A proactive approach is needed to achieve your goal. There are proven activities for almost any issue that ensure

action begins immediately. Choose the right one for your particular scenario. *These volumes outline eight activities and point to many more.* These strategic activities are from an applied behavioral scientist who has spent his life working in the field doing the very activities in this book. They work when done right, guaranteed. Yet, *activities will fail if the systemic setup is not in place for proper support.* For each activity, I will show you what must be in place to ensure results.

4. **Follow up Until You Consistently Achieve Results:** Beyond systemic setup, follow-through is where many, if not most, fail. Staying focused to achieve results is challenging and requires persistence to ensure your workplace is aligned and working toward goals. (Chapter 10 of *SOA* outlines how to follow up on tasks). Personal authority (p. 75 of *SOA*), the capability to use your personal authority (p. 218 of *SOA*), diligence, and solid structures (Chapter 8 of *SOA*) are the keys to success.

By applying these four key ingredients, you can consistently achieve high-level business results. This book is intended to help you do just that.

How to Use the Activities

The activities can stand alone, be part of a greater strategy, or be adapted to various situations. Understand and become grounded in how to do each activity; then expand and create what you need to do to develop a fully engaged culture. I offer specific ways to do things in this book, but I am in no way saying they are the only way. Once learned, adjust as needed.

Reflection and Practice

The book provides a set of facilitated processes that help create a reflective learning organization. Improvement happens through *reflection, adjustments* to the workplace resulting from that reflection, *practicing* the adjustments, and then *more reflection.*

Effective group process allows for positive cycles of practice and reflection. Workgroups, intact and cross-functional, greatly benefit from deciding to improve a process or task, practicing the new process, and then reflecting on its effectiveness. Such reflection helps determine 1) actual results, 2) potential adjustments, or 3) whether to move in a different direction. Without such a cycle 1) decisions may be made with limited information and 2) work practices, which only need slight adjustments to succeed, could be stopped. Learn how to effectively lead the activities from these volumes to improve your organization's performance.

Expert vs. Process Consultant

This book was written to train you how to help *any group* work through *anything*. It is, at its core, *a process consultant model* that provides the opportunity to teach others how to "fish" so they can continue the work themselves. This does not mean you are qualified in areas that you are not. *Process consultants* understand how to help groups *solve their own problems* by flushing out the issues, providing models, and helping the group, in the context of *systemic principles*, choose a path forward.

Expert consultants have clear answers and expertise that a process consultant does not. They specialize to help organizations solve *technical problems* or provide *content-specific expertise*.

Effective process consultants understand and recognize moments that neither you nor the group has the expertise to solve the current problem. Most organizational problems *can* be solved by existing employees, but *not all*. Learn how to tell the difference and build your integrity muscles by suggesting that the organization contract or hire a resource that you cannot possibly provide when needed.

Technology

Incorporate the latest technologies into whatever you do. I use language about flip charts and traditional styles of facilitation throughout this book. I use flip charts so all participants can see the data while facilitating effective group dialogue and when presenting new items (theories or tracking actions), to keep the last item in view. Yet, technology will continue to offer new ways of communicating.

Continue to integrate technology to increase engagement. I used phones years ago for those who could not attend meetings. Now organizations have virtual meetings with video. Perhaps the future will have holographic meetings. There is no substitute for in-person meetings, yet technology will continue to improve our options.

About This Book

This book synthesizes the work of Robert P Crosby and my years of Organization Development experience. Many of the activities presented are scattered throughout the books *Strategic Organizational Alignment; Walking the Empowerment Tightrope; Cultural Change in Organizations (CCIO); Fight, Flight, Freeze (FFF);* and *Leadership Can Be Learned.* The rest are from experiences throughout my career.

Beyond the people already mentioned, many great minds deserve credit for this book's foundation, including, but not limited to, Dr. Timothy Weber, Dr. John Scherer, Dr. L.B. Sharp, Dr. Murray Bowen, Dr. Edwin Friedman, Dr. Carl Whitaker, Dr. Salvadore Minuchin, Gilmore Crosby, John Hanlen, Dr. Jay Hall, Dr. Ron Short, and Dr. Edgar Schein.

Who is the Audience?

This book is written for those in organizations seeing the connection between increased engagement and results, yet needing a little more direction to get it right. It is for the CEO, the manager, the project manager, the organization development consultant, and others trying to engage those around them more profoundly. It is a must for functions that constantly lead groups trying to solve problems such as Quality, Safety, Maintenance, Human Resources, or Engineering, or for any external consultant.

Volume I Book Layout

Part One—Introduction. Chapter 1 summarizes the activities. Chapter 2 introduces logical ways to use events in your organization to transform your culture into a high-functioning workplace.

Part Two—Developing Intact Workgroups. Chapter 3: Transition Meetings shows how to manage transition moments, and Chapter 4: Workgroup Development is about intact work team development. *Intact work team or group means boss and direct reports.*

Part Three—Conflict Utilization. Chapter 5 addresses employee-to-employee conflict, while Chapter 6 addresses boss–employee conflict.

Part Four—Facilitator Fundamentals. This section outlines specific skills needed to facilitate or lead all the activities in Volume I and Volume II. The chapters are Facilitator Basics, The Facilitator Triangle, and The Leadership Questions. These chapters are intended to help further understand how to effectively lead sessions.

The appendices contain the theories and extras needed to lead each activity. They are presented in the way I give them during sessions, including the actual words at each step of the presentation, rather than an in-depth theory analysis. Each theory is simple, practical, powerful, and intuitive; meant to frame sessions; and aid in group reflection, awareness, and interaction. My objective is to provide you with the tools to be successful in presenting a range of theories.

Finally, a prerequisite for any facilitator is reading my first book *Strategic Organizational Alignment*. It demonstrates how authority works within systems and a systemic diagnostic tool that identifies the sponsorship scenario needed to build an effective strategy in any situation. These two core frames help facilitators effectively lead any group session.

Volume II focuses on system-wide implementations. The four activities in Volume II are group-to-group conflict, goal alignment, process improvement, and project or major initiative. Additionally, Volume II includes the keys to breaking dysfunctional workplace silos and how to build your implementation competency.

♦♦♦
Section One
Introduction
♦♦♦

CHAPTER 1

Overview

The capability for self-reflection is essential for learning. Workplaces need avenues to improve on big picture and basic items such as "I have the materials and equipment I need to do my work right." This chapter provides an overview of how to build your organization's capacity for self-reflection, self-correction, and problem resolution to increase performance and results.

This chapter focuses on strategic activities which, when adapted effectively to your organization, will create a more functional culture and increase bottom-line results. The activities use systems thinking, group process, and organizational theory to achieve your desired outcomes. This list represents the types of activities that have consistently created organizations with record business results and high employee morale. The activities ensure 1) productive work relationships, 2) clarity of goals, 3) successful projects, and 4) effective processes.

In Robert P Crosby's book *Cultural Change in Organizations (CCIO)*, he used a story to illustrate a change strategy that encompasses these activities. The following section shows the short form of that approach, as represented in Appendix B of *CCIO* and adapted to this book.

Peter's Change Strategy

- The leader sets *measurable* goals.
- Help direct reports *align* with the goals and be open to feedback.
- If your workplace has a union, work closely with union leaders and hourly employees to understand the goals.
- Communicate the goals across the organization in small groups through a *dialogue*.
- Expect the leaders of intact groups (boss and direct reports) to sharpen their goals with input from their direct reports.
- Cascade a group process in each intact workgroup as taught in Chapter 4 (or Chapter 3 of Volume II). The process must include clarity of goals, generation of issues and solutions, and follow-up.
- Work with the company's most important cross-functional (matrixed) projects and ongoing cross-functional tasks.
- Develop a critical mass of strategic employees with high interactive skills who have the capacity to take a stand and stay connected, deal constructively with disagreements/conflict, be decisive, and stay the course against resistance.
- Develop a team (cadre) of key people trained in the strategic engagement activities in this book who will help sustain the shift in culture and alignment around the leader's goals.

Peter realized he could easily turn this into a program—a new "flavor of the month"—rather than developing effective leadership.

- He reviewed the "Eleven Do's And Don'ts for Those Who Are Serious about Change" (Appendix A, *CCIO*).
- He re-read "What It Takes to Pull off a Cultural Change" (Appendix C, *CCIO*).
- He committed, in a new way, to follow up. The words "You are not serious about change until you are serious about follow-up" helped Peter realize he had been too passive when conducting follow-up. He committed to hold himself and his direct reports to higher standards and instructed them to do the same throughout the organization.

- He reaffirmed the need to have skilled internal or external staff doing day-by-day nurturing until his cadre was developed. They would then sustain the ongoing change that is constantly needed in a productive environment: managing emerging conflicts, making continuous contributions to work-process improvement, ensuring decision and role clarity, encouraging accurate data flow, and fostering authentic healthy interaction.

Peter's plan touches all critical areas needed to create and sustain whole-system change. Change strategies should be based on each unique situation and comprised of core activities, such as those in Peter's plan.

This chapter briefly explains the core strategic engagement activities necessary to move a culture. Subsequent chapters include the agenda and step-by-step instructions for each activity.

As-Needed vs. Yearly

This two-volume set is not meant to be prescriptive. It is a guide to create a successful culture. Each strategic activity that follows can be used as is or adapted to your unique situation. They fall into two categories: as-needed and yearly.

As-needed activities are intended to achieve a stated outcome, such as getting a group to function at a higher level as fast as possible or to solve an immediate problem. One such problem is conflict between groups, sometimes called *silos*. Another problem is conflict between employees that are struggling to perform.

Yearly activities are predictable moments that require effective group process to ensure system alignment, high employee engagement, and a culture that continues to learn.

As-Needed Strategic Engagement Activities—Volume I

Chapter 3 – *Transition meetings* are a structured group activity to ease the transition of either a new manager or a group that has many new employees. This model is based on the US Navy's research and is outlined in Chapter 3. US Navy research shows that workgroup effectiveness is disrupted for many months during a transitional period to a new boss and shows that a structured approach greatly reduces lost transition time. If done well, this model is reliable and effective to help workgroups stay focused during transition.

Chapter 5 – *Employee–employee conflict* occurs when two employees are in a conflict that threatens productive work. This type of conflict resolution is between two employees, neither of whom has direct authority over the other. That is to say, neither is the other's boss.

Chapter 5 outlines a process that, when done effectively, consistently solves the conflict, eases tension, and, most importantly, ensures success. Allowing ongoing conflict is a common problem in organizations, and is often the case because managers don't have a systemic frame (see Appendix C) nor trained resources to effectively manage the situation.

Most people think in individual terms and, therefore, assign blame to one party or the other rather than thinking in systemic terms. If this is occurring, then the immediate manager(s) of the employee(s) is allowing conflict to fester.

Chapter 6 – *Manager–employee conflict* provides a systemic approach to improve employee performance when the concern is other than technical. The aim is to catch employees before being placed on a performance plan.

The activity results in employees improving most of the time. If the employee still struggles, then there will be no surprises if they end up on a performance-improvement plan through Human Resources (HR). The goal is no surprises but also honesty. That is, if an employee is struggling, it is likely, at least partially, that there is a relational problem between the boss and employee. For instance, most bosses can be more behaviorally specific about expectations.

Therefore, manager–employee conflict gets clarity in two directions: 1) what specifically should the employee improve upon to raise performance and 2) what the boss can do differently to help the employee succeed. This clarity must happen in the context that the boss has the final say on any agreements. Yet, work must be done by both to improve performance.

As-Needed Strategic Engagement Activities—Volume II

Chapter 2 – *Group-to-group conflict* management is critical when two groups that must rely on inputs from each other to succeed are not doing so, thus preventing consistent outcomes. The classic scenario in the manufacturing world is maintenance or quality to the production employees on the floor. Chapter 4 shows you how to improve group-to-group functioning or conflicts.

All workgroups depend on data and supplies to complete their task. Organizations are interrelated and depend on each other. Accurate data, efficient timing of tasks, and reliable raw materials create success. Yet when asked to rate the statement on a survey: "We get, with quality and on time, what we need to do our work (question 3 on the work team survey on p. 132)." Only one-fourth of the people say, "Almost always." The rest say, "Frequently," "Occasionally," and "Seldom." Gallup found that only "3 in 10 U.S. employees strongly agree they have the materials and equipment they need to do their work right." They further extrapolate that "by moving that ratio to 6 in 10 employees, organizations could realize an 11% increase in profitability, a 32% reduction in safety incidents and a 27% improvement in quality." Imagine the improvements if you could move it to 8 in 10.

Most look upon this as an individual problem or, worse yet, blame one group or the other. Yet both must engage to solve the problem. The basic premise for employee–employee conflict is a good place to start with cross-group conflict management. The key: the manager over both supervisors whose groups are in the conflict must insist that the two groups work it out and afterward show them the plan to solve any specific moments or issues that are causing pain.

Worker knowledge must be applied to be successful (see Chapter 9, Workplace Knowledge of *Strategic Organizational Alignment* [SOA]). Ironically, managers of the areas in conflict usually cannot solve the conflicts because of their lack of hands-on knowledge of the real problems, yet they often resist involving the employees who are actually doing the work.

Chapter 4 – *System-wide process improvement* solves problems with major processes that run across departments such as order fulfillment, on-time delivery of parts, purchasing, or any cross-functional process. The approach includes 1) a clear structure to generate data, 2) high involvement of the employees who work in each area during all phases of the improvement process, 3) clear expectations and alignment of the respective reporting managers, and 4) a consistent follow-up process.

For specific problems, you may need to hire an expert consultant or involve your IT staff to resolve the issues. The expertise is frequently in your organization. Therefore, it is critical to include the correct resources from the start. Do so and the solutions can be simple.

Chapter 5 – *Major Projects or Initiatives.* Over the years we created a large-group activity that is highly structured and produces consistent results. Why? It *balances workplace knowledge* by combining managers, technical resources, and added a large amount of people who perform day-to-day tasks (see Chapter 9 of *SOA*). Thus, it focuses the whole system toward the result.

The activity combines structured brainstorming (see Appendix E of Volume II), clarity of authority (see *SOA*), clarity of decision making (see *SOA*, Chapters 12 and 13), and implementation tools such as a project timeline, created by all, to use as a guide. The process starts with a measurable goal and time frame for completion. The goal should stretch your employees, and the consequences of failure must be known by all. These are the ingredients to motivate your employees and achieve greatness.

This process has led to furnace recovery records in a smelting plant, successful cost-cutting, R&D projects that were failing turning around, software projects completed on time and with quality, and many other results.

Cost-cutting, using this method, is counter to most workplaces where it is common to have high-level managers impose top-down means to control costs, such as banning hiring outside expertise (even if they have helped you save significant dollars), and travel (even if you miss key customer visits). Often when organizations should engage their employees to help rationally maneuver difficult scenarios, they instead resort to top-down measures that demotivate and, ironically, hurt the bottom line.

Completing projects using an effective group process takes talent, expertise, and the ability to set effective stretch goals. Setting stretch goals can be dangerous in the long run, unless they include clear structures to help participants see the path to obtaining results. Such structures create commitment and excitement in organizations. Stretch goals with no clear path leads to helplessness and frustration.

This activity engages all employees impacted to methodically solve the problem. Chapter 5 provides a step-by-step guide. See Appendix N of *CCIO* for additional information.

Yearly Strategic Engagement Activities—Volume I

Chapter 4 – *Workgroup Improvement/Development.* All workgroups achieve a certain level of productivity. Even an effective group can strive to be more efficient and productive. In today's fast-paced world, things change rapidly; those who shift and adapt will be better prepared to meet their needs.

The opening pages of this book discussed the dynamics of professional workgroups compared to professional sports teams. Effective group process, understanding and tweaking how the group works together, is the key to continuous improvement. Unless your product is so unique the world cannot compete, the only way to differentiate your company from others is to improve how well you work together to achieve results.

Chapter 4 conveys how to do a workgroup improvement activity, which should be done biannually to continually strive for excellence. The keys are clear measurable goals, generating issues to solve from the employees specific to achieving the goals, creating clarity of decision making, and follow up until intended results are achieved.

One way to gather such data is to use a survey. I use an adaptation of the survey from Robert P Crosby's *Walking the Empowerment Tightrope* to improve workgroups. It identifies 25 factors but can be tailored to the specific areas (see Appendix D for my short form of that survey).

Beware of the common traps of using a survey. The most critical rule was created by Ronald Lippitt: "Those who put pen to paper must be the ones to analyze the results, derive its implications, and come up with actions to improve the workplace." Ignore this, and you misuse the survey. The most common error: give a survey and not allow those who take the survey to see the results or, worse yet, decide what they mean and impose solutions to problems that only the people who put pen to paper fully understand.

Yearly Strategic Engagement Activities—Volume II

Chapter 3 – *Goal Alignment* is a once-a-year process to align and engage employees to achieve their goals. Goal alignment is a cascaded process that starts with the lead team and continues throughout the organization (see p. 54 of Volume II). It provides a structured way for employees to understand the current state of the business, clarify measurable goals, raise issues in the way, and create solutions to achieve the goals.

Many organizations do very little to align their workforce to goals. Perhaps they release yearly numbers or create a high-level A4 (a lean manufacturing tool to focus on goals). Employees are rarely told the current situation facing their business, their department's bottom-line goals, or which process(es) must be improved to achieve those goals.

This lack of communication impacts employees much greater than many understand. Those that do not make the connection between their daily tasks and how they impact the overall organization have a much greater chance to stop using their neocortex and start functioning entirely with the limbic system (emotional area of the brain). Thoughts such as "I can hardly wait to get out of here" or "This task is so stupid" result from a lack of connection to the neocortex.

Excellent goal alignment has a cumulative effect in any workplace and engages your employees to enhance their performance.

Developing Your Employees

Clarifying the vision, managing tense situations, driving tasks to completion, working across all areas of an organization effectively, helping employees hurdle obstacles, tuning in to employees to gain clarity and understanding, making sure there is focus versus distractions, and so on are all functions of leadership that can be taught. It is every leader's job to assess how their employees, salaried and hourly, are doing in these areas and provide the expectations and means to execute them effectively.

Training in emotional intelligence is a must for today's workplace. Avoidance of issues costs organizations millions each year. Robert P Crosby created an experiential training to help leaders and employees develop such skills. There have been many versions: from a Master's program to a shorter two-week, in-house training for employees at all levels. For a larger list of skills that can be taught, see page 19.

How to Determine What Is Needed in Your Culture

The strategic engagement activities outlined in this chapter represent a list that has been proven to create high-performance, high-morale cultures that consistently achieve record numbers. That, however, doesn't mean that all workplaces should do all activities. You must decide based on your unique situation. The next two categories will help you decide.

Are You Achieving Your Business Results?

If the answer is no, then reflect on your organization and ask yourself, "Where are we most dysfunctional?" Start with the appropriate activity outlined in this chapter. Make sure you use a facilitator who understands systems thinking related to organizations as explained in my first book, *Strategic Organizational Alignment*, and then begin your journey.

Is There Tension That Gets in the Way?

Unnamed, countless managers have said, "There is no place for emotions at work" or "I don't make decisions using my emotions" or "Stop whining and get over it!"

The irony about the above statements is that they are all emotionally charged. Perhaps about fear of emotions! The reality is that humans are primarily emotional beings. Top neural scientists suggest that the amount of neural pathways from the limbic part of the brain (the area responsible for emotions) is 100-to-1 compared to the amount that comes back from the neocortex (the area responsible for cognitive thinking, reasoning, differentiating right and wrong, and decision making). The neurons travelling from the limbic to the neocortex are much stronger, like super highways, compared to the neurons travelling from the neocortex to the limbic, which are more like winding country roads. The limbic brain sits on top of the reactive brain, or brain stem, which is the part of the brain that controls your bodily functions and contains the fight/flight/freeze response to perceived threats, whether real or not.

Workplaces are emotional breeding grounds. If your employees cannot work together because they get stuck in analysis/paralysis (a cool way of fighting that appears to be logical but is a reactive state) or they have more overt fighting and disagreement, then you will need many of the engagement activities discussed in this chapter.

If two groups or departments are not working well together, then there is a strong likelihood that many of the aspects of my first book are out of whack. The rule is to work on clarity of roles, goals, expectations, decisions, and inputs first (see Appendix C), and then use some version of Chapter 2 of Volume II that will help people work better together. If tension is still high, then use either Chapter 5 or Chapter 6.

Conclusion

Increasing engagement and getting better business results is not rocket science. The activities presented in this chapter are tried-and-true. If done well and combined with knowledge of Sponsor/Agent/Target/Advocate, you will get solid results. They represent the core foundation to engage your people differently to ensure success. You can adapt and change them to suit your needs. If performed well, then expect significant improvements on all key indices.

The following chapters explain each activity, and Part 4 addresses the core facilitation skills needed to successfully conduct each one. Each chapter outlines a specific activity, the systemic setup to achieve success, step-by-step agenda and detailed explanation, and countless tips and tricks.

CHAPTER 2

Strategies for Engagement

Are you using your leadership program to transform the dynamics of your workplace or to solidify the current state?

The ensuing strategic activities can be used to improve two individuals in conflict, intact workgroups, or cross-functional processes or projects. Taken individually you can quickly gain perspective and improve, even in difficult situations. However, taken as a whole, these activities can transform your workplace into an engagement culture that will not only yield better business metrics but significantly improve the *attitudes*, *beliefs*, and *perspectives* of your employees.

Identify Workplace Dysfunction

Use these activities to engage your employees and move your work place toward greater effectiveness. Excellence requires a thorough strategy. Reflect on your workplace dynamics and intervene strategically to become more productive. Each activity serves a purpose and impacts your organization differently. Therefore, how they are applied determines the end results. The conflict chapters will help you move through various systemic stuck points, yet dysfunction in organizations often becomes the norm and sometimes seems inevitable rather than a choice.

Regardless of your workplace dynamics, *it is a choice of the leadership* to continue the path or change them. I am not downplaying the difficulty of changing dynamics. Yet, I have seen situations where departments or fractions of the workplace were not functioning or, as Gallup calls it, were actively disengaged only to become highly functional as a result of strategically engaging the workplace in many of these core activities.

Measurable goals, aligned leadership, strategic engagement activities, execution, and consistent follow-up are required to resolve dysfunction. I often see dysfunction allowed in workplaces or, worse, condoned by managers who either avoid conflict moments or manage them in limited ways such as separating the two parties. The following statements are real.

"Do not talk to anyone in X department."

"We will not participate in that improvement."

"My lawyer says, 'You cannot talk to each other until we do a full investigation.'"

"You cannot stop and help that department."

"Of course the Union will not be part of our new leadership development program."

"We cannot involve the people who do the work in this problem-solving session because they will not really participate."

Despite your current situation, the decision to become more functional is mostly a choice. If you do not use such moments and make claims such as They are not ready, The problem is not me; It is X, or That person has a "psychological" problem, then you are allowing yourself to be a victim of your current situation and your whole system is static. You are also stuck in individual "pop" psychological thinking. Most often, but certainly not always, employees who are perceived as interpersonally difficult lack specific clarity about what is expected of them. If you do not attempt to improve your workplace dysfunction either when creating a new training or by avoiding the most difficult issues between workers or departments, make sure it is a conscious choice rather than a knee-jerk reaction based on a dysfunctional workplace or your own discomfort with confronting difficult issues.

Many decide how to roll out new initiatives based on the current dysfunction and therefore solidify that dysfunction. Instead, strategically use new programs, problem-solving sessions, meetings, or initiatives to move your whole system toward more engagement and productivity.

Workplace dysfunction happens over time and is easy to see as fixed in place. Before creating a new leadership program, processes, policies, or training, think about your organization's current dynamics. What areas are highly functional and dysfunctional?

Do you have tension between

- Union and management
- Production and maintenance
- HR and *X*
- Designers and quality
- Developers and purchasing
- Finance and accounting
- Any two groups who must support each other
- Direct service and support
- Project managers and *X*
- Safety staff and *X*
- People in leadership positions and lower layers in your organization

What areas of your workplace must continue to work well or improve to reach your business objectives? Any new engagement activity or leadership program will impact your workplace one way or another. Therefore, use such moments to move toward greater organizational health, become more functional, gain more productivity, break dysfunctional silos, and reverse long-standing dynamics. It is the savvy leader who recognizes dysfunctional workplace norms and uses each appropriate moment to shift those norms toward a more functional workplace.

The Applied Behavioral Scientist vs. The Popular Psychological Model

Psychology has many benefits, yet humans who are not trained in psychology tend to use a popular version that negates greater workplace functionality. They label groups or employees in a way that solidify the current state.

Applied behavior science is the branch of psychology that permeates this book. The applied behavioral scientist removes barriers to whole system health by removing the inflammatory rhetoric that surrounds behavior and invites dysfunction.

Evaluative statements about readiness, while impossible to avoid, often keep businesses from improving. If you think the lead team is not ready, or the Union won't do it, then you are in a psychological model and may be defeating your attempts to upgrade the organization. Those opinions or judgments must be continually challenged and tested.

The activities in this book are focused on the whole system and come from applied behavioral science and systems thinking, which states that as you impact the environment, you will create positive behavioral changes. Seize the moment when creating anything new to move the organization toward health. Make sure you do not inadvertently solidify the current dysfunction in your workplace.

Program Creator or Strategist?

Are you a program creator or a strategist? Programs are created to accomplish a task. Strategic engagement activities are created to change the current dynamics and move the whole system toward greater productivity and health.

Consultant: "Why are you coming to this training?"
Participant 1: "Oh, well, actually it is November and I need to fulfill my yearly training quota as directed by the company policy."

Consultant: "Why are you coming to this training?"
Participant 2: "Oh, well, Joe, my boss, said I need to come to the training to apply what you are teaching to our mission-critical project. In fact, he will join the training. The project has experienced serious resistance, and we want to create a strategy for success."

It is easy to see which participant will benefit from the training.

Using Strategic Engagement

Intervene to solve problems that rights wrongs, heals wounds, and fixes business dysfunction that is negatively impacting productivity. This approach creates a higher purpose connected to your events.

Wade into conflicts to move the organization toward health and end dysfunction. Employees who refuse to speak to one another and other conflicts in organizations are like a "disease" with no cure. But they can be cured because the methods, means, and ability have always existed. Once you own this reality, the trigger becomes the choice to learn how to respond differently in key moments to solve the problems. This is true no matter your role, yet the role of manager is extra critical (see p. 119 of *SOA*, The Role of the Leader in Conflict Management).

Engagement Is Not a One-Time Event

Ongoing persistence is required to change workplace dynamics, especially for long-standing dysfunction. However, ongoing dysfunction can quickly improve with effective strategy and strategic engagement activities.

Organizations tend to return to old patterns. To achieve real change the workplace must be aligned effectively and maintained over time. Furthermore, persistence and effective follow-up ensure successful outcomes even if the initial event is mediocre. Ineffective follow-up can destroy great beginnings.

To impact workplace engagement and move toward greater health, you must establish more functional ways to gain worker input and generate healthy dialogue.

Align the Leadership

Strategic activities should be created by the business leads and driven through the organization by an aligned lead team. This requires strong leadership from the top as many department heads may prefer to remain in the dysfunctional patterns already embedded in the workplace.

If you hire a HR or training professional to establish a training or leadership development program, they must use constant dialogue with the lead team to ensure they set forth a strategy that closely aligns with the goals of top management and moves the whole system toward greater productivity and health. Training and activities are not solely for the purpose of individual learning, though that is important, but to help the organization become more skilled in achieving its goals.

If HR or any function develops a plan that is allowed to be imposed on the workplace with little or no dialogue, the likelihood of success decreases and the probability of over-functioning is high. However, if a plan is built, supported and driven by the organizational leaders directly over the employees impacted, then you can move mountains.

Components of Engagement Strategy

Use the following components when building a strategy.
- What problem are you trying to solve?
- What is the measurable goal(s) (see Appendix E).
- Who does the day-to-day tasks where the problem exists?
- Who are the best technical people to assist?
- Who must work together to accomplish the task?
- What groups work well together?
- What groups do not work well together?
- Read Chapter 9 in SOA to ensure you balance workplace knowledge.

What processes are too cumbersome?
- Think about it and be honest; do you really need five signoffs for a $5 purchase order? Or nine signoffs on a contract?
- Has your workplace fallen into the trap of trying to overly control behavior through imposing processes? Or the opposite, do you have no process(es) where you obviously need one?

Let your imagination dictate your direction and act now!
- "Our workplace would be better if . . ."

Reflect on the above questions that apply to your situation (add any others that you think would help), then build a strategy to achieve your business results and increase morale.

Emotional Intelligence

These activities are the building blocks to create a healthy culture. Consistent and strategic use will yield positive results. Create an aligned workplace as taught in *SOA*, and then use the right activities to engage your employees toward your goals.

However, some workplaces are stuck in dysfunctional patterns and need extra help. These workplaces require emotional intelligence (EQ) skills that use behavioral models and interactive skills to get beyond stuck, defensive, toxic, and contentious work teams. In those situations, it is critical to build your workplace's muscle in basic interactive skills to do the following:

- Move from a stance of "victim" to that of "creator."
- Move from blaming to owning one's part in any transaction.
- Move from arguing to having a dialogue (tuning in to the other).
- Move toward integrating thinking with feeling and getting more in touch with one's emotions, which influences all decisions.
- Move from generalities to specifics and become more able to separate descriptions from interpretations about work processes and relationships.
- Move toward speaking for oneself—saying "I" when "I" is accurate, "you" when "you" is accurate, and "we" when "we" is accurate.
- Move from being inflexible and predictable in tense situations to having multiple options of how to be in those moments and the ability to apply them.
- Move toward being a leader who will take a stand and (a seeming paradox) listen with more empathy.
- Learn key systemic principles that apply to interpersonal communications, day-to-day tasks, and all change.

You must be strategic when adding leadership or EQ training. Groups that do not work well together should be in the same scheduled training. The best model is to train in EQ and then follow that training with any number of activities in this book. The trainings must be clearly sponsored and presented with specific reasons of *why this* and *why now*.

Conclusion

Creating the right activities and trainings in your workplace is only part of the task. Use these activities and trainings to create strategies led by the business leaders to help your organization move toward higher engagement, better functioning, healing old wounds, and ultimately, improving productivity.

◆◆◆

Section Two
Developing Intact Workgroups

◆◆◆

CHAPTER 3

Transition Meetings

Almost all workplaces are in transition. Employees leave for one reason or another and each departure has an impact. There is a step-by-step way to significantly reduce downtime when there is a new leader or new employees. What follows is a simple and repeatable activity that accelerates productive work in moments of transition.

Introduction

The act of saying, "I am leaving my position" sends a wave of emotions throughout a work team and often an organization. That wave is proportional to how respected or disliked that particular leader is among the employees. Studies by the US Navy indicate that periods of transition are filled with certain characteristics partially because the future becomes less known than the immediate past.

1. High uncertainty/low stability.
2. High levels of "inconsistency" (perceptual).
3. High emotional stress on people.
4. High energy (often undirected).
5. Control becomes a major issue.
6. Past patterns of behavior become explicitly valued.
7. Conflict increases, especially intergroup.
8. Productivity decreases.

Figure 1 Characteristics of a Transition State

Research conducted by the US Navy documented a consistent decrease in effectiveness and productivity lasting approximately six months (see Figure 2). However, downtime can be reduced through a structured transition. After applying this approach, research showed a reliable reduction of the disruption period from six months to around a month when applying an effective transition strategy.

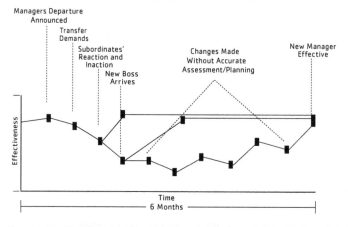

US NAVY ORGANIZATIONAL TRANSITION CHART
(Top to bottom order of line on chart)
Downtime when transition work occurs with both old and new manager
Downtime when transition work occurs with new manager
Downtime due to transition state with no assistance

Figure 2 The Transition State

A transition meeting is a facilitated conversation between the subordinates and the new leader as soon as possible (or during high turnover between the leader and new employees). The process is relatively simple and helps the leader and employees learn about each other, the current work situation, and the new direction, if any, and to explore how to effectively work together. The US Navy conducted their meetings as soon as the new officer came aboard.

Much is learned when conducting such a session. If it occurs on day one, the group will accelerate immediately, focus on the current issues, begin learning about how to work together, and understand the expectations of the new manager. If the session occurs one month later, then employees can clear up gaps or confusion beginning to emerge in their working relationships. The group process involved in a transition meeting means that the employees have their concerns, issues, and questions answered at the same time. If this meeting does not take place, then learning how to work together and addressing pressing issues happens at a much slower rate.

Preparation

Best practice in terms of preparation for transition meetings is a three-part process. 1) The former boss and new boss overlap a few weeks so the new boss can learn from the old. 2) The facilitator meets with the new boss before the meeting to review the transition meeting agenda, learn about any support needed during the meeting, hear any concerns, and strategize to address potential emerging issues. 3) The facilitator interviews the employees one by one to help orientate them to the process, learn about current issues, teach concepts like decision clarity, and build rapport.

Prepare the Boss: Review and explain each stage of the agenda. Help the boss prepare to deliver the opening statement and determine the outcomes they want to achieve during the meeting. For instance, at the start of transition meetings, many bosses share their background and experience to add context about how they may manage. Coach the boss to request openness and ensure no retribution to employees who raise difficult topics. Confirm if the boss needs help with any blind spots (e.g., listening during tense moments).

If this session is part of a strategy driven by the organization's leadership, perhaps developed and derived from Chapters 1 and 2, then part of prepping the boss can be education in core theories and ways of interacting being used in the organization (see *SOA* and the appendices in this book for potential core theories).

Interview the Employees: Review and explain each stage of the agenda. Help employees begin to determine issues to address during the meeting. Help employees shift their language about difficult topics to behavioral specifics to ensure constructive dialogue. I often do not interview employees for transition meetings, as they are a "nice to have" but not critical.

Facilitator Preparation: Read the following: Chapters 7 and 8 for basics in facilitation, the core triangle in tense moments, plus the concepts of neutrality and reciprocity; Chapters 8 and 12 of *SOA* for structure and decision making.

Length of Activity: Meeting lasts four hours, but could take longer for larger groups.

Room Setup: One flip chart and pens. Arrange participants to ensure eye contact, as facial expressions help create dialogue. Advanced technology may alter your approach to capturing actions and behavioral expectations. Ensure the actions, theories, and commitments are easily visible to all participants as aids to understanding and dialogue.

Core Mental Models/Skills
- Transition Theory (p. 24)
- Victim/Creator ("I" Language, Appendix B)
- Behavior Description (Chapter 4 of *FFF*)
- Decision Making (Chapter 12 of *SOA*)
- Accountability (Chapter 7 of *SOA*)
- Follow-Up (Chapter 10 of *SOA*)

Step-by-Step Agenda

1. Opening Statement
2. Introduce Facilitator
   - Introductions
   - Overview process
   - Facilitator role
   - Transition theory
3. Generate Discussion Topics
   - Boss leaves
   - Groups develop lists
     - Work in groups of two or three
     - Questions to *Ask* the boss
     - Statements to *Tell* the boss
4. Group Dialogue
   - Boss returns
   - Dialogue (each item captured on the lists)
   - Facilitator charts two lists
     - Behavior expectations
     - Action items (Single Point of Accountability [SPA], What, and By-When)
5. Close

Agenda Explanation

Opening Statement: *The manager starts the meeting* by sharing hopes for the day, addressing meeting protocols and logistics, and sharing pertinent information with the employees.

Meeting Protocols:

- Expectations of participants.
- Put away all electronics (cell phones and laptops).
- Emergency procedures (safe meeting location).
- Ask for openness about the current work team situation. The manager must be clear that there will be no retribution if difficult topics are discussed. That expectation can only be fully ensured by the manager's boss (their Sponsor), yet the facilitator can ensure the whole system remains connected. Openness is critical to an engagement culture. Setting the stage and building trust with one's manager is an important part of these activities. Difficult topics must be addressed appropriately and resolved if possible, which builds trust and creates greater openness.

Brief sharing by the boss could include:

- Positions held at other companies.
- Education.
- Philosophies that guide their management style.

(Optional) Facilitator Task during Opening Statement: *Opening Dialogue*—After the manager's opening statements and before the employees respond, have the employees *turn and talk* to the person beside them about the following:

- Any *comments* or *questions* for the boss before we start?

This is optional because some may be meeting the boss for the first time. Regardless, they are just developing a working relationship. Therefore, *if the boss does not say much during the opening, move to the next task without dialogue at this stage.*

Why have people turn and talk? An engagement culture engages all employees. If you do not provide structured dialogue, then you will likely only hear from the extroverts. This small act breaks the typical patterns in the organization and gives everyone a voice. This task is a long-standing pattern breaker. Most have learned in school and at meetings that they can sit passively and not engage. Your task is to break that pattern and gently push the culture to interact.

The wording of the question is intentional. Always ask for *comments* or *questions.* If you only ask for questions, then employees may twist their statements into questions. When that happens conversations get more complicated and indirect communication patterns are more easily formed.

Introduce Facilitator: The facilitator provides pertinent information about their background and then meets all the participants (if interviews were not possible). The facilitator sets expectations about how they will help in tense moments and in other moments will add structural, cognitive, or behavioral theories to ensure effective outcomes. I typically say, "Please speak for yourself, and if tension arises, I may slow things down by asking one of you to repeat what you think the other said." Setting expectations is important to ensure people understand the process and, if tension does arise, are ready to do something different when asked.

After discussing expectations, review the agenda and the theory of transition meetings. Conclude your introduction by stating the primary purpose, which is to reduce the downtime of effectiveness of working relationships when a new boss starts managing a department.

Generate Discussion Topics: The group creates a list of items to ask or tell the boss. Typically the boss leaves the room and I give the following progression of instructions. When the boss leaves, instruct the employees to develop items they want to be discussed during the meeting.

The following progression is deliberate to generate maximum information presented constructively to ensure healthy dialogue.

1. **Step One**
   - Work in pairs
   - Develop two lists
     - Questions you want to *Ask* the boss
     - Statements you want to *Tell* the boss

At this time, I hand out the Potential Transition Topics (p. 35) to help stimulate the thinking process. Then I give the pairs 20 minutes to generate topics. Also, I remind them to raise all important topics, which may or may not include anything from the transition topic list.

2. **Step Two**
   - After a few minutes, remind each pair to list all items regardless of whether they are in agreement. The act of pairing is *not intended to be an act of creating consensus*, but rather to fully engage each group participant, build working relationships, and have a partner to help generate topics.

3. **Step Three**
   - After 20 minutes, check each group's list. Coach the participants to change any interpretive word into a behavioral specific (see Chapter 4 of *FFF*). I sometimes allow them to illustrate their topic, but I do not want any harsh judgments, as it will create a predictable argument unless it is being said to a savvy and highly emotionally intelligent boss.
     - This step is the key to the kingdom for constructive conversation and a real engagement culture. Work cultures that do not engage do so, at least in part, because they are unclear about the distinction between a judgment and a behavioral specific. Consequently, employees that have tried to have difficult conversations have typically led with a negative judgment. This approach creates tension and increases the odds of a poor outcome. Most struggle to remain constructive when an employee raises a difficult topic by starting with a negative judgment of them.

Alternate Data Collection Method: Once the pairs finish their initial lists, capture the list as a group on the flip chart. Go pair by pair, with the facilitator writing one item on the flip chart at a time, per pair, then capturing the next item from the next pair. The facilitator continues around the room until all items are captured. If pairs have duplicates, they are marked off their list. This method allows the facilitator to ensure all items are addressed and uses the wording of items to help teach the group about behavioral specifics. Thus, the group learns that skill together. The downside is that it takes extra time before the manager returns and the dialogue starts.

When you use this method, you must also add a discussion about who presents the data to the manager. Here are your choices. 1) The person who raised it says it. This may seem like a logical choice, yet many have the same item on their list, and in some situations, raising this question helps the employees build their fear of too much openness. 2) Have a spokesperson start the conversation and then involve those who share the issue in the dialogue. The problem with option two is that it lets employees pass on starting a dialogue by speaking directly to the boss. Only use this option as a last resort in moments of high tension. Tell the group the process is option one, and only add option two if needed.

This chapter is continued with the nontraditional data collection method where each pair's list remains with them. I raised the alternative data collection method because it has merit. Use it when the situation benefits from extra control by the facilitator, such as when there is high tension between the boss and employees.

Group Dialogue: When the boss returns to the room, prepare for the dialogue by giving the following guidelines.

- Explain *reciprocity* and that you will track actions and behavioral expectations.
- Start with the first pair raising a topic.
- After that topic is worked in the group, move to the next pair and continue around the circle until *all* items are worked. You will likely go around the circle multiple times.
- Each item brought forth is intended for the entire group to generate discussion.
- To start the dialogue, encourage *the employee* who wanted the issue/item on the list to *say it directly to the boss.*
  - ○ ***Beginning facilitators often fail at this moment.*** The core concept is about who gives the data to whom. *This moment is key to developing an engagement culture because it teaches employees to be direct even if the issue is difficult or complicated.* Use these moments to help employees build the capacity to talk directly to their boss about issues no matter how apparently difficult. This increases trust and deepens the boss–employee relationship. Gallup confirms that the key to an engagement culture is strengthening the working relationship between boss and employee. Because transition meetings are typically filled with less difficult topics as other meetings, like workgroup

development meetings (see Chapter 4), they present a great opportunity to build confidence and strengthen the boss–employee relationship. An engagement culture allows all layers to talk directly to each other, and all issues can be worked directly. This is not to say it is a free-for-all. In fact, clearly aligned leadership is critical for an engagement culture. Yet, the core tenet is the ability to speak directly to each other in nonjudgmental and therefore behaviorally specific ways.

Thus, this group will practice doing just that.

- The first task of the boss when the employee raises an issue is to *listen* and *articulate their understanding* of the item as behaviorally specific as possible. Then a constructive dialogue ensures each employee adds what they think, responds to each other, fills the gaps, and eventually the group works toward potential solutions.

Transition meetings are typically about how to effectively work together. Working larger issues is more likely to occur during work team development sessions, as outlined in Chapter 4.

During the dialogue your task is to help the group interact as constructively as possible by focusing on the following:

- Help the conversation go from general to specific. Meaning, notice discussions that start or remain at the judgment or interpretive level and help guide the conversation to specifics. Do so by asking for illustrations, specifics, or what the other said or did. For each general statement, the speaker normally has a specific example in mind. Do not allow the group to waste time arguing judgments or generalities.
- State decision making process. The conversation is, at its heart, a consultative process between the boss and employees.
  Meaning, the employees have influence, yet the boss has the final decision.
- Track actions and behavioral expectations using task component clarity (see pp. 51 and 52 for examples).
- Encourage participants to speak for self ("I" language).

- When tension rises, use the John Wallen *skills* to help people connect and slow down the conversation.
- If employees are talking about people in the room, then help them talk directly to the person. The mental model is called *triangulation.*
- If the boss struggles to create an action that is clear, then provide assistance by stating what you think is the action.
- If the boss is assigning themselves most of the actions, then help them delegate actions appropriately.
- If an employee is nervous to mention something that you think may not necessarily be a big issue, then support the employee to raise it and have a constructive dialogue.
- Notice employees politely waiting for their turn that others do not notice and call on them (gate keeping).
- Help the boss slow down if they are creating actions too fast before learning enough from the group.
- At the end of the dialogue, ask if you can do all this given your current resources? If not, what actions shall be delayed?

Close: After all items are discussed, use the following process to rate the session.

1. Make small pieces of paper or use 1 1/2-inch Post-it notes.

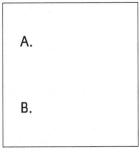

Figure 3 Example Small Survey

2. Use a flip chart to duplicate Figure 4 (see next page).
3. Distribute a small piece of paper to each participant.
4. Tell them to:
   a. Write down letter *A* and *B* as shown.
   b. Do not include your name.
   c. The purpose is to receive semi-anonymous feedback.

5. Ask the following questions:
   A. What is your confidence level that we raised the right issues?
   B. What is your confidence level that we created the right actions and behavioral expectations to address the issues?
   Rate each on a scale of 1–10 with 10 being high.
6. When completed, fold your survey and pass it around the room. At some point say, "OK, now all of you need to have a survey, and if you get your own, just don't tell anyone." Occasionally somebody will say, "Oh I got my own," but it really doesn't matter.
7. By a show of hands, write the number on the flip chart corresponding to each score. This immediately rates the session.

Confidence level that we:

Raised the right Issues

Lo   Hi

| 1 | 2 | 3 | 4 | 5 | 6 | 7 | 8 | 9 | 10 |

A. | | | | | | | | | | |

Created the right Actions

Lo   Hi

| 1 | 2 | 3 | 4 | 5 | 6 | 7 | 8 | 9 | 10 |

B. | | | | | | | | | | |

Figure 4 Closing Survey Scoring Sheet

Ask the group if anyone would like to say any closing words. Offer the manager to have the final comments. The meeting is now finished.

The closing process of rating the meeting can be used to *rate any session quickly* and is a nice way to get all the opinions visible immediately. The process also serves as a gut check for those who often complain after the session. It is harder to take one negative voice seriously if most rated a session an 8 or higher. In the unlikely event that the scores are low, it provides an opportunity to ask the group what issues or actions were missed.

Potential Transition Topics

Credentials

- What is your background? What skills and knowledge do you bring? What degrees/education do you have?
- What do you want us to know about you?
- Do you prefer more "hands on" or "hands off"?
- What type of behavior is necessary to be effective while working with you?

Basic Communication and Policies

- How should we communicate with you? By e-mail? In person? By phone?
- Do you hold work team meetings? How often? Past meetings were effective/not effective?
- How do you handle vacations?

Solving Issues/Problems

- If I have a problem, how much data do you need? How would you prefer to receive it?
- Can I bring you issues that I do not know how to solve?

Structure

- How are decisions made? Who is consulted before the decision? Who is informed after the fact? Who can veto a decision?
- I can/cannot make decisions that I need to do my job.
- There are a few decisions that I have to wait for someone else to make, in which I wish I could make myself.
- Our workflow is working/not working.

Current Issues

- Our workgroup is running at X efficiency.
- The major issues are X and Y.
- These are the organization's key strengths and weaknesses.
- These things interfere with my job.
- How do you function as a team? What is your role in the team?
- I hope you change this part of our culture.

Work Team Input Needs

- As a team we get/don't get tools/info/support to do our job.
- Our internal suppliers/customers work well/poorly.

Employee Utilization

- I have X skills that are not being used.
- Our department is structured effectively/not effectively.
- Person task fit is working well/not working well in our job.

History

- I want to conserve this part/none of how we were functioning before your arrival. Life here has been easy/difficult. Here is the story of the last 10 years.
- These are the informal rules that determine how things really get done.

Difficult Moments of Disagreement (Conflict)

- How would you describe your conflict style?
- If I disagree with you, can I tell you? In public? Behind closed doors?

Accountability

- How do you hold your people accountable?
- Our past boss always/never/rarely supported new initiatives or critical daily work by gaining clarity of direction and holding people appropriately accountable.
- There is/isn't a single point of accountability for each role, task, and action.
- Actions always/never/rarely get done on time, and when slipping, people always/never/rarely notify others that they will miss the date.

Options

Transition sessions can also be adapted. If there is a new CEO and you have a savvy facilitator, then you can use the basic principles of this activity to engage with all employees in various settings. This offers an efficient way for the CEO to learn about the employees and organization from the people themselves and an excellent platform for the employees to quickly connect with the new CEO. To do so, give instructions, have employees turn and talk, and then start fielding comments or questions. Larger impromptu meetings allow fewer opportunities to prepare for constructive dialogue. Therefore, the facilitator must be versed in behavioral specifics to help the manager address less-than-perfect questions or comments.

Conclusion

Transition sessions are a simple and powerful way to remove anxiety and confusion when onboarding a new leader. Use these sessions to accelerate a group's effectiveness. The best practice I have seen is for the manager's boss to require them to meet with the Organization Development (OD) professional and schedule a transition session immediately. Engagement should not be a choice; it should be an ongoing practice.

CHAPTER 4

Workgroup Development

Perhaps the most powerful way to ring the cash register is to develop each intact workgroup. This chapter conveys the step-by-step process Robert P Crosby used to transform multiple organizations. Adapt the process to any situation and consider teaching it to internal resources for ongoing use.

Introduction

Self-reflection is essential for learning. Many intact work teams (boss and their direct reports) should spend more time thinking about their current situation, develop ways to be more successful, implement actions based on their insights, and follow up until they are consistently obtaining better results.

This chapter illustrates a step-by-step process to improve your work team. You will learn an effective way to understand most issues your employees think are hampering their productivity and quickly turn them into action. When done well, actions will be distributed to the appropriate person, boss, or employee. *This is not a dump on the boss.* The process at heart is a consultative decision-making process where the boss has the final say.

Like Chapter 3, work team development sessions focus on direct feedback by using a specific process to help ground issues, allow employees to improve, and help the boss lead with more clarity.

Apply this chapter's process at least once a year to each workgroup. Making small corrections by involving your employees is critical for all workgroups and key to developing an engagement culture. If you do not maintain employee-engagement activities, regression is likely.

The work team development process outlined uses a survey (see Appendix D). Workplace surveys can increase or decrease morale. Decreases often happen rapidly. The following process ensures maximum positive benefit from any survey.

Rules of Using a Survey

"We know what does not work. It does not work to survey people and not show them the results. It also does not work to survey people and have top management or an outside expert develop recommendations (prescriptions). It does not work to survey people and have a general session and report the results to all concerned and do nothing else. These approaches all have been tried hundreds of times and, with rare exception, been found wanting. People become irritable and defensive, with a resulting lowered morale and decreased work efficiency."

—Robert P Crosby

"Employees who complete surveys have a fundamental right: They who put their pencil to the survey paper should also see and work the data."

—Ronald Lippitt

1. Administer survey to all targeted employees (intact groups).
   - If all employees take the survey, make sure it is separated to each workgroup. Also, make sure each workgroup gets their own data and the comparison mean of each question to the larger organization.
2. Have employees complete the instrument.
   - Strive for 100% participation.
   - Have employees complete the survey semi-anonymously.
   - Do not allow written anonymous feedback.
   - Inform the employees that they will not only see the results of the survey but also analyze it and create solutions to improve their workplace.
3. Score the survey.

4. Give the scored survey to the employees.

5. Let the employees raise issues based on their interpretation of the data, beyond the words of each question, to specific work issues that need addressing.

6. Capture the issues on flip charts and dialogue with the boss about which to solve. The boss has the final say (i.e., consultative decision-making style).

7. Develop distinct actions to solve each issue making the final list.

8. Ensure balance so that the employees and boss have actions.

9. Study, learn, and help deploy reciprocity (see p. 81).

10. Add SPA and By-When. The SPA for each issue must be with the work team, and must be given appropriate time and resource help to achieve success.

11. Follow up on actions until issues are solved. Create new actions, as needed, if original action proves unsuccessful to solve issue.

The Problem with Anonymous Feedback

The goal of an engagement culture is to allow all employees to be fully open about what is working and not working within the organization. Anonymous feedback does the opposite, as it allows for indirect feedback to rule the day and may create a dependency within your organization on "expert consultants" to help interpret the data.

Anonymous feedback allows indirect triangles to live in your organization. The intention of anonymity is to make it safe for all to give feedback, perhaps from managers who struggle hearing dissent. Yet, all too often anonymous feedback contains harsh judgments rather than behaviorally specific data. The practice encourages indirect behavior, propels bosses to guess or be suspicious about who said what, and hurts the ability to learn in the giving and receiving end of the feedback process.

Instead of allowing anonymous feedback through various processes like 360 feedback, written responses on yearly employee surveys, or suggestion boxes, create an ongoing process of open feedback using the various methods in this book. Make sure no one can give feedback anonymously. *If managers in your organization give retribution when difficult topics are raised, then ensure their bosses hold them accountable* through appropriate consequence management.

Anonymous feedback is a process to protect people when managers are not properly managed. Processes do not manage people; people do. Managers who reprimand employees for raising difficult topics create disengaged workplaces. Feedback then becomes underground and more indirect. Instead of creating anonymous feedback practices, effectively hold your managers accountable to build a culture of engagement.

Survey feedback, as explained in this chapter, creates a direct culture within the boundaries of your authority structures. It provides a platform toward being open and direct so managers and employees can build stronger work teams.

Being Better Employees

This activity challenges the manager and their direct reports to become better at having constructive conversations about work issues that are hurting productivity and effectiveness in the work team and turning those conversations into action.

Managers are provided an opportunity to build their engaged leader capabilities with help from a trained facilitator. This includes an invitation to hear directly from each employee-specific areas of improvement to create a better workplace. The facilitator aids the interaction to ensure understanding between the manager and employees and then helps the manager turn the conversation into an action or new expectation, if appropriate.

Direct reports are provided an opportunity to build their engaged follower capabilities with help from a trained facilitator. This includes raising issues they think must be addressed to reach the work team's goals and saying them directly to their boss in a group setting. The facilitator aids the interaction by helping each employee state their issues in behavioral rather than judgmental or interpretive terms to ensure a successful conversation and ensuing dialogue.

Preparation

Best practice to prepare for a work team session is a two-part process. 1) The facilitator interviews the boss before the meeting to explain the meeting format, learn about any concerns, and, critically important, prepare them to present their workplace goals. 2) The facilitator interviews the employees to explain the meeting format, help begin to identify issues, potentially teach concepts like decision clarity, and build rapport.

Prepare the Boss: Review the meeting agenda, and explain each stage. Help the boss prepare their opening statement and what they want to achieve during the meeting. Coach them to request openness and to ensure no retribution when difficult topics are raised. Discuss how you typically help during interactions within the group and then ask if there are particular moments where they would like your aid, such as listening during tense moments. Also, learn about the boss's goals for the work team and coach them toward the specificity standard set in Appendix E.

If this session is part of a strategy driven by the organization's leadership, perhaps developed and derived from Chapters 1 and 2, then part of prepping the boss can be education in core theories and ways of interacting being used in the organization. (See *SOA* and the appendices in this book for potential core theories).

Interview the Employees: Review each stage of the agenda. Help them begin to reflect on issues to address during the meeting. Help shift difficult topics toward behavioral specifics to ensure constructive dialogue. Interviews are a "nice to have" and can be done solo or in small groups.

Facilitator Preparation: Read the following: Chapters 7 and 8 for basics in facilitation, the core triangle in tense moments, plus the concepts of neutrality and reciprocity; also read *Strategic Organizational Alignment*. It is helpful to know multiple problem-solving methods as work team development sessions often identify many potential problems.

Length of Activity: Meetings last four hours with no add-ons and four employees. Add one hour per employee; a large group takes 1 day.

Room Setup: One flip chart and pens. Arrange participants to ensure eye contact, as facial expressions help create dialogue. Advanced technology may alter your approach to capturing actions and behavioral expectations. Ensure the actions, theories, and commitments are visible to all participants as aids to understanding and dialogue.

Core Mental Models/Skills

- Rainbow Theory of Goals (p. 23 of *SOA* or p. 41 of Volume II)
- Work Team Survey Questions (Appendix D)
- Victim/Creator ("I" Language, Appendix B)
- Behavior Description (Chapter 4 of *FFF*)
- Decision Making (Chapter 12 of *SOA*)
- Accountability (Chapter 7 of *SOA*)
- Follow-Up (Chapter 10 of *SOA*)

Step-by-Step Agenda

1. Opening statement
2. Introduce facilitator
   - Introductions
   - Overview process
   - Facilitator role
3. Workgroup goals
4. Group completes survey
5. Generate discussion topics
   - Score and return survey (see p. 40)
   - Boss leaves
   - Groups develop lists
     - Work in groups of two or three
       - What they want *More of*
       - What they want *Less of*
       - What they want to stay the *Same*
     - From the *boss* or *each other*
6. Group dialogue
   - Boss returns
   - Dialogue (each item captured on the lists)
   - Facilitator charts two lists
     - Behavioral expectations
     - Action items (SPA, What, and By-When)
7. Close
   - Set follow-up date

Agenda Explanation

Opening Statement – *The manager starts the meeting,* states the purpose, asks for openness (see p. xx), addresses basic protocols (see Chapter 3), and introduces the facilitator. Critical factors:

- **Sponsorship Clarity**—*Strong Sponsorship is critical in any intact workgroup meeting or activity.* The boss of the group is, by definition, the Sponsor. *The boss decides when to start, not the facilitator, which is a core moment of meeting ownership.* If a boss asks me, "Should we get started?" Especially if people are late, I always respond with my opinion and say, "This is your meeting; start when you are ready." The boss begins by stating the importance and desired outcomes of the meeting. *The boss owns the meeting, not the facilitator.* If you think the boss does not want the meeting, then consider cancelling it.

- **Fear of Retribution**—Prepare the manager if fear of retribution is present. The manager must acknowledge the fear and ensure there will be no retribution. You must contract with the boss for you to speak up immediately if their behavior appears as retribution. The objective is to slowly nurture employees to give and receive freely with no fear of (and no real) retribution. That takes time and sponsorship.

Introduce Facilitator: The facilitator provides pertinent information about their background and then meets the participants (if interviews were not possible). The facilitator sets expectations about how they will help in tense moments and in other moments will add structural, cognitive, or behavioral theories to ensure effective outcomes. I typically say, "Please speak for yourself, and if tension arises I may slow things down by asking one of you to repeat what you think the other said." Setting expectations is important to ensure people understand the process and, if tension does arise, are ready to do something different when asked.

After discussing expectations, review the agenda and the meeting's purpose. For example, "The purpose of today is to create an even more effective work team."

Workgroup Goals: The manager presents the workplace goals. Preferably the goals are numeric, measurable, and relatable to the work team. Creating numeric goals is harder than it seems. Your initial coaching on goals will help prepare them for this moment. If the manager has clear numeric goals, then the group dialogue will be about clarity and expanding them to include work process goal. If the manager needs to create initial goals, then a group conversation will help sharpen and clarify them. Ideally, the manager has well-developed goals and can simply articulate them in terms of bottom line, work processes, and key initiatives or projects.

Facilitator task during workgroup goals: *Opening Dialogue*—After the manager shares the goals and before the employees respond, have the employees *turn and talk* to the person beside them about the following:

- What do you like about the goals?
- What do you think you disagree with?
- What else do you want to learn?

Why *turn and talk* rather than simply starting the conversation with the total group? An engagement culture engages all employees. If you do not provide structured dialogue, then you will likely only hear from the extroverts. This small act breaks the typical patterns in the organization and gives everyone a voice. Plus, this actively engages all participants with content within 20 minutes of the meeting starting.

This *turn and talk* is a long-standing pattern breaker. Most have learned in school and at meetings that they can sit passively and not engage. Your task is to break that pattern and gently push the culture to interact. *The wording of the three questions is intentional.* Question two, for instance, is worded "What do you think you disagree with?" It's important for people to understand that many disagreements come from misunderstandings. This wording gives employees license to raise disagreements without believing they know they disagree with the manager. That said, another option is asking, "What are you concerned or confused about?"

Group Completes Survey: The group completes the questionnaire in Appendix D. This questionnaire is derived from a larger survey and sharpened to just the items, that if a work team does well, will yield record results. Score the survey and return it to the employees. Follow the instructions on page 40. If possible, have the participants complete the survey before the meeting, electronically or by hand.

Generate Discussion Topics: The group creates a list of issues and problems to solve to reach the goals aided, but not limited, by the survey results. Use the following progression to raise issues and generate constructive conversation.

1. **Step One**
   - Return the scored survey and explain the survey numbers.
   - Use Appendix D to explain your scoring method.
   - Have the boss request specific areas to receive feedback.
   - Traditionally, the boss leaves. When leaving, I instruct the boss to develop a list of issues to address upon returning.

2. **Step Two**
   - Work in pairs.
   - Develop three lists.
     - What you want *more of* (from boss or group)
     - What you want *less of* (from boss or group)
     - What you want to *stay the same* or maintain (praises of the boss or group)
   - Reaffirm that the list is to solve problems raised by the survey and issues in the way of reaching the goals.
   - Give the group 20 minutes and assist as needed.
   - Affirm that any topic can be addressed, even issues that are not related to the survey.

3. **Step Three**
   - After a few minutes, remind each pair to list all items regardless if they are in agreement. The act of pairing is *not intended to be an act of creating consensus*, but rather to fully engage each group participant, build working relationships, and have a partner to help generate topics.

4. **Step Four**
   - After 20 minutes, check each group's list. Coach the participants to change any interpretive word into a behavioral specifics (see Chapter 4 of *FFF*). I sometimes allow them to illustrate their topic, but I do not want any harsh judgments, as it will create a predictable argument unless it is being said to a savvy and highly emotionally intelligent boss.

- This step is the key to the kingdom for constructive conversation and a real engagement culture. Work cultures that do not engage do so, at least in part, because they are unclear about the distinction between a judgment and a behavioral specific. Consequently, employees that have tried to have difficult conversations have typically led with a negative judgment. This approach creates tension and increases the odds of a poor outcome. Most bosses struggle to remain constructive when an employee raises a difficult topic by starting with a negative judgment of them.

Alternate Data Collection Method: Once the pairs have finished their initial lists, capture the list as a group on the flip chart. Go pair by pair, with the facilitator writing one item on the flip chart at a time, per pair, then capturing the next item from the next pair. The facilitator continues around the room until all items are captured. If pairs have duplicates, they are marked off their list. This method allows the facilitator to ensure all items are addressed and uses the wording of items to help teach the group about behavioral specifics. Thus, the group learns that skill together. The downside is that it takes extra time before the manager returns and the dialogue starts.

When you use this method, you must also add a discussion about who presents the data to the manager. Here are your choices. 1) The person who raised it says it. This may seem like a logical choice; yet many have the same item on their list, and in some situations, raising this question helps the employees build their fear of too much openness. 2) Have a spokesperson start the conversation and then involve those who share the issue in the dialogue. The problem with option 2 is that it lets employees pass on starting a dialogue by speaking directly to the boss. Only use this option as a last resort in moments of high tension. Tell the group the process is option 1, and only add option 2 if needed.

This chapter is continued with *the data collection method*, where each pair's list remains with them. I raised the alternate data collection method because it has merit. Use it when the situation benefits from extra control by the facilitator, such as when there is high tension between the boss and employees.

Group Dialogue: When the boss returns to the room, prepare for the dialogue by giving the following guidelines.

- Explain *reciprocity* and that you will track actions and behavioral expectations.
- Start with the first pair raising a topic. They can raise either a *same as* (praise), *more of*, or *less of*.
- Share praises directly to the boss. There are three options. 1) Start by having each pair share a praise and continue until all praises are shared, 2) have each pair share one praise, then share a more of or less to improve, or 3) use option 1, but at the end of the meeting. *Positive feedback is perhaps the most underused feedback in organizations.* Before the meeting ends, make sure the group shares their praise lists.
- After that topic is worked in the group, move to the next pair and continue around the circle until *all* items are worked. You will likely go around the circle multiple times.
- Each item raised is intended for a whole group dialogue.
- To start the dialogue, encourage *the employee* who wanted the issue/item on the list to *say it directly to the boss*.
  - *Beginning facilitators often fail at this moment.* The core concept is about who gives the data to whom. *This moment is key to develop an engagement culture because it teaches employees to be direct even if the issue is difficult or complicated.* Use these moments to help employees build the capacity to talk directly to their boss about issues no matter how apparently difficult. This increases trust and deepens the boss–employee relationship. Gallup confirms that the key to an engagement culture is strengthening the working relationship between boss and employee.

    Intact workgroup meetings may include difficult topics that employees have avoided raising to the boss for a variety of reasons. Using a trained facilitator presents a great opportunity to build confidence and strengthen the boss–employee relationship, which is the key to an engagement culture. In an engagement culture all layers can talk directly to each other, and all issues can be worked directly. This is not to say it is a free-for-all.

In fact, clearly aligned leadership is critical for an engagement culture.

Yet, the core tenet is the ability to speak directly to each other in nonjudgmental and therefore behaviorally specific ways. Thus, this group will practice doing just that.

- The first task of the boss when their employee raises their issue is to *listen* and *articulate their understanding* of the item as behaviorally specific as possible. Then a constructive dialogue ensures each employee adds what they think, responds to each other, fills the gaps, and eventually the group works toward potential solutions.

Work team development meetings tend to create 8–15 actions and a list of behavioral expectations to improve the outputs of the team and solve their issues.

During the dialogue your task is to help the group interact as constructively as possible by focusing on the following:

- Help the conversation go from general to specific. Meaning, discussions that start and remain at the judgment or interpretive level and help guide the conversation to specifics. Do so by asking for illustrations, specifics, or what the other said or did. For each general statement, the speaker normally has a specific example in mind. Do not allow the group to waste time arguing judgments or generalities.

- State decision clarity; the conversation is, at its heart, a consultative process between the boss and employees. Meaning, the employees have influence, yet the boss has the final decision.

- While creating the action list, help the employees and boss set clear By-Whens (see Chapter 7, Accountability of *SOA*).

- Encourage participants to speak for self ("I" language).

- When tension rises, use the John Wallen *skills* to help people connect and slow down the conversation.

- If employees are talking about people in the room, then help them talk directly to the person. The mental model is called *triangulation.*

- If the boss struggles to create an action that is clear, then provide assistance by stating what you think is the action.
- If the boss is assigning themselves most of the actions, then help them delegate actions appropriately.
- If an employee is nervous to mention something that you think may not necessarily be a big issue, then support the employee to raise it and have a constructive dialogue.
- Notice employees politely waiting for their turn that others do not notice and call on them (gate keeping).
- Help the boss slow down if they are creating actions too fast before learning enough from the group.
- At the end of the dialogue, ask if you can do all this given your current resources? If not, what actions shall be delayed?

Who (SPA)	What	By When
Joe	Create training matrix complete with who, what, and by-when. With input from group, review during one-on-one's.	6/24/2017
Jane	Create form to track issues and a visual board to track % complete of machine builds.	6/15/2017
Mary	Check new database status and report during next team meeting.	6/1/2017
Tom	Talk to inside sales about new plant startup and project specifics.	6/1/2017

Figure 5 In Dialogue Tracking—Action List

Figure 5 is a partial list of actions created during a work team development session. The facilitator helps the group translate their in-depth conversations on each topic into actions or behavioral commitments (see Figure 6).

The lists in Figures 5 and 6 were created by the facilitator tracking the commitments made during the interactions between the boss and employees. It is important while tracking commitments to remind the group that *the process of work team development is, at its heart, a consultative process, where the employees raise issues and the boss has the final say* (see Chapter 12, Decision Making of *SOA*). Honesty about decision clarity is a key component of an engagement culture. The intended outcome is to help improve the boss and employees' ability to engage constructively

Behavioral Expectations

All	If other departments in the organization come to you with work or projects, take it but copy me on email.
All	If you are traveling, I want you to call and say if you need to stay, or if you are done. I will let you do what you think is right barring contractual obligations. If Tom is gone, then leave a voicemail. If you know that Tom won't be in (i.e., he is on vacation), then call Frank and Tom's boss to let them know.
All	If you have an issue with another person, then you need to tell them directly using behaviorally specific, nonblaming language.
All	If you are removed from working on a machine, then you must inform the appropriate team members.
Tom	I will create one-on-one meetings with each of you. Starting in July, I will meet with each of you one time per month.

Figure 6 In Dialogue Tracking—Behavioral Expectations

about any issue. If the process is done well, and followed up well, the group learns to be more direct and work through issues much faster. Employee influence will increase and better solutions will be implemented.

Final Review of Actions: Review the action list and ensure that the wording is clearly an action, verify the dates, and confirm or adjust resources. Adjustments could mean reducing actions, changing dates, changing SPA, or additional actions.

Close: See page 33 of Chapter 3 and close the same way.

Beyond the closing process, ensure that the manager schedules a follow-up meeting. The date should depend on the following:

- How much pain exists in the workgroup?
- What dates are on the action list?

A typical time frame is about 6 weeks, but that could be adjusted based on the various factors. If the session is part of a system-wide activity, then the date may be preset so the boss just has to inform the group.

Follow-Up Process: This process takes about two hours. Once the meeting starts, I normally say something like "OK, I have a simple process to go through to work these issues. A major step in follow-up is simply having them. So give yourself credit for just being here. Now, I want you to rate the actions and commitments from the work team meeting on two dimensions." Use the following process to rate the issues and expectations and generate constructive conversation.

1. **Step One:** Pass out commitments
   - Hand each person a copy of the commitments and actions.
   - Have them number each commitment and action.
   - Have them draw a line on the right-hand side of the list creating two columns (see Figure 7).
2. **Step Two:** Rate commitments
   - Rate each action or expectation on the following dimensions:
     - Are they done?
     - Are you getting the intended results?
   - Rate both dimensions on a scale of 1–10, 10 being high.

While participants are rating, they often say, "How can I rate this, I do not know anything about it?" If so, I add extra rules such as "OK, if you do not know but you need to, then write a zero. And, if you do not know and do not need to, then you can leave it blank. However, I prefer you stretch yourself and give your opinion on each one."

#	Who (SPA)	What	By When	(1-10) Done	(1-10) Results
1	Joe	Create training matrix complete with who, what, and by-when. With input from group, review during one-on-one's.	6/24/2017	5	3
2	Jane	Create form to track issues and a visual board to track % complete of machine builds.	6/15/2017	7	5
3	Mary	Check new database status and report during next team meeting.	6/1/2017	1	1
4	Tom	Talk to inside sales about new plant startup and project specifics.	6/1/2017	8	6

Behavioral Expectations

#	Who	What	Done	Results
5	All	If other departments in the organization come to you with work or projects, take it but copy me on email.	8	9
6	All	If you are traveling, I want you to call and say if you need to stay, or if you are done. I will let you do what you think is right barring contractual obligations. If Tom is gone, then leave a voicemail. If you know that Tom won't be in (i.e., he is on vacation), then call Frank and Tom's boss to let them know.	6	6
7	All	If you have an issue with another person, then you need to tell them directly using behaviorally specific, nonblaming language.	4	9
8	All	If you are removed from working on a machine, then you must inform the appropriate team members.	9	10
9	Tom	I will create one-on-one meetings with each of you. Starting in July, I will meet with each of you one time per month.	10	7

Figure 7 Follow-up Example

3. **Step Three:** Gather the data
    - Go one question at a time around the group.
    - The first person reports their score and you capture it on the flip chart; then go to the second person and continue until you have captured all scores for action 1.
    - Only allow participants to report the numbers.
    - Move to action 2 and repeat the process.
    - Be disciplined and do not allow explaining during this step. Tell the group that dialogue is the next step.

This method only takes a few minutes to gather the data. Stick with the rules by gently reminding them that each item will be discussed during the next step. Figure 8 illustrates an example of the final numbers.

Item #	(1-10) Done					(1-10) Results				
1.	8	1	8	7	5	3	5	1	6	3
2.	6	1	8	7	7	3	5	1	3	5
3.	7	1	1	3	1	3	1	1	5	1
4.	9	1	1	8	8	3	5	1	6	6
5.	9	0	8	10	8	3	0	9	7	9
6.	6	1	8	7	6	3	5	1	6	6
7.	6	1	8	7	4	3	5	1	6	9
8.	6	1	8	7	9	3	5	1	6	10
9.	10	9	10	1	10	7	6	10	1	7

Figure 8 Follow-up Compiled Ratings of All Employees

This engagement tool helps employees increase openness (p. xx) about what is working and not working. It gives equal airtime to all employees and a quick visual rating of each commitment. The next step is to have a dialogue to understand what is underneath the ratings. Apply the following rules for the dialogue.

- If many actions, then apply the rule *ask* or *tell*.
  - Go to the action that you want to learn, and *ask* a question.
  - Go to the action that you want others to learn about and *tell* them what you want them to know.
- If a small amount of actions, then address each item.
- Hear explanations from the SPA who worked on the action.
- Learn from others about the action.
- Talk about what is working and not working.
- Generate or adjust actions as needed.
- Review the section "During the dialogue" on page 50.

Effective follow-up is a dialogue intended to continue momentum toward lasting solutions. Many solutions need small tweaks, and some actions may need to be added or deleted. Formal follow-up allows for reflection, decisions on actions, and engagement from employees to ensure the right course is taken to achieve the goals.

Success Variables

The two biggest success factors of this event are how well is it *sponsored* and how effectively it is *followed up*.

Sponsorship is multidimensional. If the session is self-generated and condoned by the boss, then sponsorship, by definition, is in. If the manager's boss mandates the session, then that boss must clarify the importance to the manager. If the manager does not want the activity, but the boss says it must be done to solve specific items, then the event can still be successful.

A common mistake is to think improvement only happens if the person wants it. Strong sponsorship from the right person means *the manager does not have to like it but is willing to do it.* Leaders must use *generative power* to ensure growth is not optional in organizations, yet many avoid such conflicts (*SOA*, p. 71).

The second factor is follow-up, which requires formal and informal follow-up. Each leader must work the action list from the beginning and use "The Fundamentals of Follow-up Check List" to ensure effective informal follow-up (*SOA*, p. 149). At least one formal follow-up should happen as explained on the previous pages.

Optional Add-ons

This activity can be adapted to meet whatever needs you are trying to achieve by additional developmental theories. My favorite add-ons are Appendix A, SOCIAL STYLE and Appendix B Victim/Creator.

SOCIAL STYLE explains internal tension and blind spots that may or may not be happening in the group. It is perfect for intact workgroups. The most striking example was when a group was talking about one machine creating half of the scrape in the plant and costing millions per month. One participant suggested to study the machine for the next several months to understand the issues, yet many in the group already articulated specific pain caused by the machine. I then stated, "According to the SOCIAL STYLE chart on this lead team, you will talk about this for months, maybe years, and not make a decision." (See an example SOCIAL STYLE systemic chart on p. 120.) The SOCIAL STYLE chart placed almost all the lead team members in either the Analytical Style or Amiable Style quadrant and none in the Driving Style quadrant. At that point the plant manager said something like, "Wow, OK I am going to put in an RFA tomorrow to replace the machine."

Victim/Creator is profound in its ability to focus on self-improvement versus blaming other groups. "Fix our house first before complaining about the neighbors," as one client told his direct reports. This does not exclude raising issues that are truly about working better with other groups as remedies to input or output needs.

Add a section between introduce facilitator and workgroup goals called "workgroup development" or the theory name. I normally name Victim/Creator, "culture of accountability" because I have them focus on core items regarding accountability in the context of the conversation.

System-Wide Option

Workgroup development sessions are perhaps the most powerful way to shift a culture and rapidly improve business results. Apply the same type of cascading process illustrated in Chapter 3, Goal Alignment of Volume II (p. 54).

Start with the lead team and conduct a session *with every group* within a few weeks. This requires strong sponsorship from the Initiating Sponsor to ensure 100% participation and the proper follow-up that allows an organization to achieve its goals. The system-wide option quickly addresses systemic issues plaguing all workgroups.

Prepare the lead team managers to cascade the sponsorship throughout the whole system by 1) educating them on what will happen in each work team, 2) selecting any add-on theories for each group, and 3) working through issues with the boss, the Initiating Sponsor.

Potential systemic issues that may be discovered:

- Broken or dysfunctional processes (too many signoffs or steps, or inconsistent results as identified by the employees)
- Lack of priorities
- Broken equipment
- Role clarity issues
- Various unresolved conflicts (group to group, employee to employee, or boss to employee)
- Failing projects

Conducting this system-wide allows your employees, within a clear structure, to rapidly diagnose and solve issues. Some issues will be so large that the organization will need a bigger strategy, as presented in Chapter 2, Group-to-Group Conflict, Chapter 4 System-Wide Process Improvement, and Chapter 5, Major Project or Initiative all in Volume II. **Working with a Manufacturing Floor:** Different considerations should be applied when working with 10 or more employees on a manufacturing floor. See page 52 in Volume II to apply a different structure and agenda to address the issues.

KRID

System-wide workgroup development is perhaps the biggest bang for your buck in terms of rapid culture change toward increased results and improved morale. Start by cascading the process to each workgroup and then help the organization manage the issues that arise by building sponsorship at the right levels and using a variation of the process called KRID. KRID stands for Knowledge Retrieval Implication Derivation (see Appendix B of Volume II). Apply the following KRID after all workgroups complete their sessions. Prepare a large room and have all managers and other key people join the closing process (end of initial work sessions).

1. **Step One:** Whole group reviews work session outputs.
   - Review list of session ratings. (See closing ratings. The facilitator must save each one.)
   - Review master list of SOCIAL STYLE. (Take pictures and put dots on the SOCIAL STYLE grid color coded by work team.)
   - Review total list of actions (by having the actual flip charts of lists or an Excel sheet of all actions per group) and ask these questions: Do we have too many actions based on our resources? Are there duplicate actions and if so, are they necessary? If unnecessary, which person in what group should take the action?
2. **Step Two:** Share in small groups.
   - Talk to each other in small groups (3–4) to discuss learnings, share issues, and clarify actions raised in each session. After 5–10 minutes, switch groups and repeat. Continue until all participants have interacted, if possible.
3. **Step Three:** Derive implications.
   - Pair and derive implications to the organization.
   - Suggest actions and decide in a consultative conversation with the Initiating Sponsor in the room.

Combine this with other activities in the book to improve multiple places in an organization in short manner. The short form survey used in this book is derived from Robert P Crosby's book *Walking the Empowerment Tightrope*, which is also a guide to solve workplace problems. Of course, the activities in this book are not the only way to achieve an engaged culture. Use them with other methods you may have learned, such as Lean, Six Sigma, or other problem-solving means. Once the organization is aligned as defined in my first book, *Strategic Organizational Alignment*, then all problem-solving methods become more effective.

Conclusion

Workgroup Development is a simple, practical, and repeatable way to help a group self-reflect and improve. Groups usually have the tools to resolve their own problems. Apply this process to help translate 360 or inflammatory, employee-engagement processes into sessions where employees learn to give direct feedback. Learn this method in-depth and then adapt it to fit your needs. It is perhaps my most used tool.

◆◆◆
Section Three
Conflict Utilization
◆◆◆

CHAPTER 5

Employee–Employee Conflict

The health of any workplace is determined by how effectively conflict is utilized. A core awareness for all leaders is to realize that managing conflict is a choice and is more about leader behaviors than their employees in conflict.

Introduction

Chapters 5 and 6 (and Chapter 2 in Volume II) provide models that can be applied in various conflict situations. This chapter is devoted to conflict between two employees who have no legitimate authority over each other.

Were you surprised when you just read that managing conflict is a choice? This point is critical. You cannot choose whether conflict exists. Conflict exists in every workplace. However, you can take advantage of the opportunities presented by these moments to better your organization. The amount of conflict happening day in and day out varies in each workplace. See Appendix F: Conflict Climate Index and Appendix G: Emotions at Work to reflect on your workplace and implement structures to effectively manage conflict.

What is the difference between workplaces that manage conflicts better than others? They are honest about the existence of conflict and have an effective means to manage such moments to reduce dysfunction. Many workplaces fail to provide effective structures to manage conflicts and do not instill the proper sponsorship to ensure the structures are implemented. Conflict is often systemic in nature because employees in tension are caught in unintended systemic pinch points. Failure to raise awareness and provide platforms for conflict management allows ongoing systemic dysfunction. Finally, some managers, aware or unaware, believe that adults should get along and they should not get involved. This belief helps them avoid conflict (see Chapter 14 of *SOA*).

Systems Thinking and Conflict

This model is systemic and removes the typical pattern of conflict, which focuses on who is right and wrong. Instead, this model holds the employees and the whole system around them accountable to work through the issues or misunderstandings. A skilled facilitator, armed with the lessons in this book and *Strategic Organizational Alignment*, can highlight and raise the systemic issues that may have initially caused the conflict.

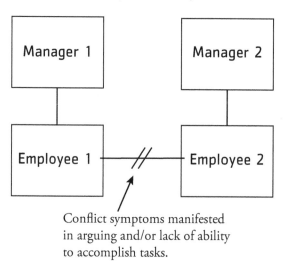

Conflict symptoms manifested
in arguing and/or lack of ability
to accomplish tasks.

Figure 9 Typical View of Conflicts Between Employees

Conflicts are often the result of two managers, out of alignment, giving their employees competing expectations and/or priorities. This common dynamic is rarely intentional. Gaining real alignment requires dialogue, which takes time, and hence most people inadvertently skip it. Figures 9 and 10 illustrate this dynamic.

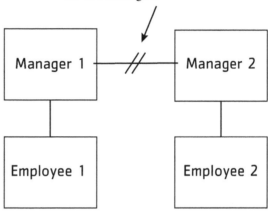

Conflict happens because of unresolved systemic issues such as conflicting expectations, priorities, or lack of clear decision processes. Therefore, the real conflict is between the two managers.

Figure 10 Systemic View of Conflicts Between Employees

The third-party conflict-management process that follows addresses this potential dynamic. Third-party facilitation means that you are helping two or more people work through a conflict in which you are not personally involved. However, facilitators can only solve these points if they are *trained* to identify systemic issues and are *sponsored* to gather the right people to solve them. To that end, see Chapter 7, Facilitator Basics which includes core competencies, and Appendix C: The Waterline Model. Third-party work using a whole system focus 1) manages conflict so tasks become more productive, 2) ensures maximum learning from each party in the conflict and how they contributed to the issue, 3) resolves the systemic issues that created the conflict, and 4) creates a plan to handle similar situations in the future. *Openness to managing conflict tremendously helps organizations improve.*

Facilitator Preparation: Read Chapters 7 and 8 to understand the facilitator triangle in tense moments, plus the concepts of *neutrality* and *reciprocity*. Use of *self* to ensure direct and constructive communication holds the key to this activity.

Length of Activity: Approximately two hours for each individual meeting and 2–4 hours for the actual meeting with the two parties.

Room Setup: One flip chart and pens, and ensure participants face each other (see Chapter 8).

Core Mental Models
- The Interpersonal Gap by John Wallen (Chapter 3 of *FFF*)
- The four key skills of John Wallen, especially Behavior Description, Paraphrase, and Perception Check (Chapter 4 of *FFF*)
- VLOMP (p. 98)
- Decision Making (Chapter 12 of *SOA*)
- Accountability (Chapter 7 of *SOA*)
- Follow-up (Chapter 10 of *SOA*)

Step-by-Step Process

I. **Systemic Setup:** Build appropriate sponsorship for the conflict resolution. Meet with the boss of each employee and clarify that they expect the employees to improve their working relationship. Do the following:

A. Coach the boss to say the following (the boss is the sponsor or, as outlined in *SOA*, the Sustaining Sponsor).

1. Tell each employee that they don't have to like each other, but they do have to work well together.

2. I am using a consultant (or name the internally trained third-party facilitator) to work through the problems.

3. Share specific consequences if not successful (as discussed in Chapter 6: Manager–Employee Conflict, the consequences must be real).

4. Outline the specific tasks or problems for which the employees must develop a plan to manage more effectively.

If the boss of either employee does not care if the conflict is resolved, then do not go forward. It is a setup to believe that people should "just get along like adults" when there is no sponsorship by either boss (i.e., if either boss does not want this work done, then the employee of that boss will likely stay loyal to them).

II. **Interviews:** Before each interview, confirm that the sponsor has talked to each employee, set expectations for the conflict resolution, and informed them that you will be the third party. Meet individually with each party to the conflict. Include the following interview components (do steps A, B1, and B2 and then the rest of the meeting can be more circular).

A. Confirm that the employees talked with the sponsor and verify the message. If the conversation did not happen, then stop immediately and involve the sponsor.

B. Explain your role as a facilitator.

1. You will lead the process.

2. You will not be an arbitrator and resolve the issue.

3. You will, to the degree possible, balance the power among the individuals in the conflict (e.g., between an hourly employee and a department supervisor).

4. You will help the parties reach agreements with "By-When" dates.

5. There will be follow-up sessions to ensure agreements are implemented by both parties.

6. The focus will be on future behavior, not on attempts to determine who was right or wrong in the past.

C. Allow the individual to ventilate feelings and judgments. During the original venting, coach for concreteness by helping each employee change general statements (judgments/inferences) into behavioral specifics.

1. Each time the individual reaches a behavioral specific, say, "When we meet with X (the person with whom they are in conflict), use specifics and not generalities."

2. Coach them to express emotions in a nonblaming way. Spend as much time as necessary and only meet with both parties together if you think the participants can speak in a nonblaming, specific manner.

D. Get a verbal commitment that they are committed to improving the work relationship with the other individual. Tell them they will start the session by making a commitment to each other.

E. Encourage the individual to be specific about the problems with the other party (what, where, how, when, and why).

F. Take minimal notes. Remind the individual that you are preparing them to *raise their own issues* during the interaction with the other. If the participant raises critical issues that must be addressed, then contract with the individual to share it if not discussed. Then write it down so you remember (memory is rarely perfect).

III. **Third-party Meeting:** Conduct the meeting (2–4 hours).
  A. Opening
    1. Explain the facilitator's role.
    2. Get a recommitment from each individual (spoken directly to the other party) that they are committed to improve their working relationship.
  B. Interaction between parties
    1. Process steps for effective interaction. See page 98 of Chapter 8 and use the process steps for VLOMP. Although the steps are sequential, once the dialogue starts, it will likely be a circular interaction that moves between steps.
  C. Closing
    1. Make clear that each party is responsible to track their own agreements, plus that a written copy will go to each boss.
    2. Set a time and date for the first follow-up meeting; within 1 week if the problem is critical.
IV. **Follow-through:** Follow-through is critical and must happen in a few ways.
  A. Informal
    1. Share the commitments immediately with the bosses (sponsors) to help them gain clarity and understanding. This can be done alone or, preferably, with the individual(s) in the conflict.
    2. Highlight any systemic way in which the boss added to the conflict. Systemic issues like role confusion, competing expectations, or lack of decision clarity are common in interpersonal or intergroup conflicts.
    3. Finally, coach the boss to monitor the commitments until it is clear the conflict is managed effectively.
  B. Formal
    1. Conduct at least two follow-up meetings. Base this on the severity, duration, and intensity of the conflict. If severe, the follow-up must happen weekly for a few weeks. If mild, then less frequently.

2. Process for follow-up meetings
  a. Review and rate each agreement. Are the commitments being followed, and are you getting the intended results? Make adjustments where necessary.
  b. Check if new issues have surfaced, and set new agreements if needed.
  c. Schedule the second and third follow-up meetings.

A note about second-order change

Throughout this work, focus on the immediate agreements (first-order change) and patterns between the two individuals (second-order change). Do the latter by insisting that the individuals speak to each other directly—not through you. The goal is that long after the original agreements are achieved, the two individuals interact with each other in a new pattern, enabling them to solve new problems as they arise or prevent potential problems.

Frequency of Follow-Up Guidelines

The following illustrates how frequently to follow up after a third-party conflict. This includes boss–employee, employee–employee, group, and group to group. The frequency of follow-up is based on the following and advocated by the third-party facilitator.

- How troubled is this work relationship?
- How long has trouble persisted?
- How frequently do the participants interact during a given day?
- What is the proximity of the participants (i.e., same office or in a separate location)?
- Was either participant behaving from a wounded place? If so, provide extra support.
- How emotional was the third-party session?
- How clear are the behavioral commitments from the session?
- How committed are the bosses to ensuring the session works?
- How healthy is the whole system in which they are working?

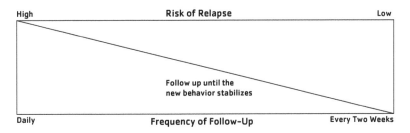

Figure 11 Frequency of Follow-up

Use these factors to decide if the risk of relapse is high. The higher the risk, the more frequent the follow-up until the participants demonstrate behaviorally that they can consistently overcome the same moments that they struggled with before the work.

I have learned, painfully, that when I do not recognize the right risk factors, I do not strongly advocate for appropriate follow-up. In those cases, the whole system dynamics will return the participants to their dysfunction. It is also predictable that the participants will blame each other if a relapse occurs.

Effective follow-up leads to learning, tweaking commitments, and reinforcing excellent work. If left untreated, and the situation is volatile, then people will likely slip in the wrong direction.

Conclusion

Work conflicts can help work through systemic issues while creating a more productive environment. Establishing a resource for ongoing third-party work in your organization allows managers an outlet to be more direct about conflict that hurts productivity. Additionally, you provide a platform to enable employees to grow, and the whole system can uncover unintended pinch points.

CHAPTER 6

Manager–Employee Conflict

"I could stand no more, so I finally put X on a performance plan"
—countless managers
"I cannot figure out my manager."
—countless employees

Introduction

This chapter's activity is used as a best practice in some organizations before placing any employee on a performance-improvement plan. It was created by Robert P Crosby and first presented in his book *Cultural Change in Organizations*.

Consider this scenario, which I have seen in many organizations—a manager has not been satisfied with an employee's performance for a long time. The manager then puts the employee on a performance-improvement plan, which surprises the employee. In other words, the manager was disappointed for quite some time yet hoped the employee would improve without having to say anything. This common practice is illustrated in Figure 12.

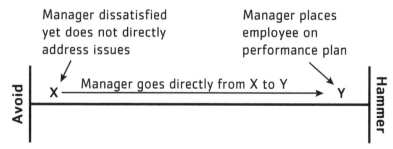

Figure 12 Common Employee Management Practice

Now consider the dynamics of putting an employee on a performance-improvement plan. Normally it happens with the employee's manager, a Human Resources (HR) manager, or another HR employee. Notice the power dynamics. The employee knows they are being reprimanded by their manager and the HR manager, who controls hiring and firing. The employee realizes the boss has authority. Include the HR manager and there is a tremendous power imbalance. The situation is set up as a one-way interaction with little or no learning taking place.

This chapter presents an alternative model based on systems thinking. The focus is the relationship between boss and employee and the lack of clarity that has been allowed to persist. In this model, if the employee is not performing, then the boss assumes they have not been clear about expectations. Performance is viewed through a systemic lens, which al- lows for greater learning to take place by boss and employee. Systemic issues like SATA, role clarity, and decision clarity are raised and resolved.

The boss starts by saying, "I have not been clear. I need to clarify my expectations of what you need to do to succeed. I also want to learn about anything I am doing that is hindering your productivity." This uncommon *systemic* practice is illustrated in Figure 13.

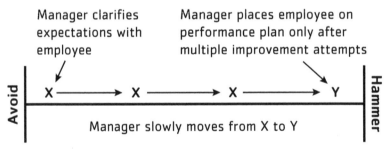

Figure 13 Systemic Improvement Practice

This practice allows the manager to learn to lead with more clarity and provide the employee extra support and ample opportunity to improve performance. Therefore, employees are not surprised if, eventually, they are placed on a performance-improvement plan. When organizations apply this as a standard practice, 1) employees improve, 2) managers improve, 3) and organizations save money from not training new hires

This model's systemic lens holds all accountable. Yes, the employee is not performing, but the boss is also not being clear. If it does not work, then the steps are in place to put the employee on a performance-improvement plan. No employee should be surprised when put on a performance-improvement plan.

Don't use this model in situations where the boss is convinced the employee is technically unable or truly does not want the employee to succeed. Also, use caution if the manager is not willing to see this as, potentially, a systemic rather than personality problem. Meaning, the manager may be part of the problem. That is, you may have a troubled work relationship rather than an employee problem.

The following scenario illustrates two ways of thinking.

Among the mechanics in your shop, it's clear that Mike is viewed as a problem employee. Dealing with Mike directly presents you with the following possibilities.

Option A: Bring Mike in for a talk, making it clear what Mike must and must not do for his work to be considered satisfactory. Initiate disciplinary procedures so he understands that you mean business.

Option B: Meet with the group to determine what is and what is not working well. Specifically, explore if people get the information and materials they need and have the proper decision authority to perform at a high level. Find how clear they are about their tasks and priorities and if they are able to significantly influence the purchase and repair of equipment, materials, and other resources needed to do their job.

Option B was the systemic option. If option A is your usual pattern, then you may be caught up in the twentieth-century culture of individual psychological motivation. If so, it is highly unlikely that your efforts to boost productivity, quality, and morale will achieve the level of success you want for your workgroup.

How Systems Problems Create Poor Performance

Data analyzed from more than 600 companies isolated certain organizational factors that lead to stress.

Key Factors

1. Lack of decision authority for my responsibilities.
2. Lack of clarity about my role.
3. Lack of clarity about my role in the rest of the organization (I am often asked to do things outside my role).
4. Lack of specificity in performance evaluation or feedback.
5. Lack of understanding of the larger picture about where my department and company are going.
6. Not being appreciated for outstanding work.
7. Lack of influence over things that affect my work and areas of experience and expertise.

It's ironic that managers spend untold hours on so-called "problem employees" rather than deal with systemic issues that create a stressful environment. An hourly worker in a manufacturing plant reported that the yearly department grievances dropped from 200 to 30 after implementing systemic approaches and improved conflict-management skills.

Let us assume that you've solved the systemic dilemma and still think it is a troubled employee issue. From here it is simple. Follow the process that starts on the next page. If done well, the employee will succeed most of the time. In the rare occasions they do not, you'll have documentation to do whatever is within the authority granted by your organization and its policies.

Examples of Not Being Specific About Relational Goals		Examples of Specifics by Two Supervisors Demonstrating Different Interpretations and Unique Expectations
Take more initiative.	*May mean*	"Come into my office almost every day with fresh ideas to explore."
	Or may mean	"Come back in a month and tell me what you've done."
Be cooperative.	*May mean*	"Tell your peers what you have been doing and request their input."
	Or may mean	"Don't bug peers with your project unless asked."

Figure 14 Examples of Not Being Specific About Expectations

Facilitator Preparation: Read Chapters 7 and 8 to understand the facilitator triangle in tense moments, plus the concepts of *neutrality* and *reciprocity*. Use of *self* to ensure direct and constructive communication holds the key to this activity.

Step-by-Step Process

I. Manager clarifies expectations

A. Write your expectations. Specify what you want technically and relationally.

B. Share your draft with a neutral third party to help translate judgmental words into specifics.

II. Inform your employee: Meet with your employee to establish the improvement process. Specify your beliefs and wants as follows:

A. You are not satisfied with the current level of performance.

B. The performance must improve to a satisfactory level (use numeric metrics if possible).

C. You will do all you can to help the employee succeed.

D. If performance does not improve by a specified date, then you will apply consequences (consequences must be within your boundaries and followed through, or your workers will never trust your word).

E. Explain that "it takes two to tango" and you play a role in the performance issue. Therefore, you met with a third party for assistance to ensure your expectations are behaviorally specific.

F. You also need help to understand your part in the low performance. Therefore, your employee must also meet with the third party to understand what is needed from you to succeed.

III. **Employee prepares for meeting:** Have your employee meet with the third party. Ask the employee, "What do you need from your boss to be successful?"

A. Employee generates a list.

B. Third party helps convert each item into behavioral specifics.

IV. **Manager–employee meeting:** Meet with your employee and the neutral third party to share both lists.

A. Clarify your expectations.

B. Ensure you understand the employee's requests.

C. Make appropriate commitments. Agree to change behavior stated in specific terms. With bosses and employees, this is not an equal-among-equals conversation. The boss may insist on items that the employee might not be happy about, but of course, the more collaboration in the agreements, the better.

If the third party is neutral but also a high-level manager, then the employee could hesitate to open up because of the power imbalance.

V. **Follow-Through:** A plan for effective follow-through is critical. The plan consists of three types of follow-up: formal, ongoing, and long term. All three must be incorporated to ensure success.

A. Formal Follow-up: Have two formal follow-up meetings, like outlined below, at a minimum. Base this on the severity, duration, and intensity of the problem. If severe, the follow-up must happen weekly for a few weeks. If mild, then less frequently.

1. First meeting: Schedule 2 weeks out for the follow-up, a "throw-away" evaluation. Note success and failure and reclarify expectations and commitments.

2. Second meeting: Meet 2 weeks later for the second formal follow-up. No "throw-away" this time. By now, the die will be cast. You will know. Nine times out of 10 the employee will succeed. One in 10, in my experience, will not.

      a. Process for the follow-up meetings:

          i. Review and rate the list of agreements. Are the commitments being followed, and are you getting the intended results? Make adjustments where necessary.

          ii. Determine if other issues have surfaced, and set up new agreements if needed.

          iii. Make plans for the second and third follow-up.

  B. Ongoing: Pay attention on a daily basis that you are keeping your commitments. Waiting for formal follow-up is not acceptable.

  C. Long Term: Schedule a periodic meeting to check status and ensure continued success.

A note about follow-up—if you create a good process and skimp on the follow-up, then do not blame the employee for failing. If the relationship has been highly contentious and the problems lingered for years, then you must have more follow-ups. You must then consistently reinforce the agreements, including 1) successes with positive, informal feedback, 2) instantaneously address relational "pinches" that arise, and act fast to try different solutions on failed efforts. Paradoxically, if the result of your clearly stated expectations and direct, clear communication with the employee leads to the turnaround, then the problem was not a troubled employee but a troubled relationship. It may also be a whole systems problem. Look for other employees who lack the necessary clarity.

Conclusion

Manager and employee dynamics are complicated for many reasons. Some factors are due to individual history, organizational misalignment, and competing interpersonal patterns. This relationship is the most critical when creating an engagement culture. Do not allow a one-dimensional view of solving problems rule the organization's behavior when managers struggle with their employees. Instead, hold all parties accountable and try to learn about other systemic forces at play. Use each moment of conflict to help your organization increase its ability to learn and improve.

◆◆◆
Section Four
Facilitator Fundamentals
◆◆◆

CHAPTER 7

Facilitator Basics

I am just a facilitator. What can I do?

Introduction

The word "facilitator" is often used in such a way to indicate that just about anyone can do it. To effectively create an engagement culture, facilitators must have some basic skills to help move a workgroup while ensuring their own blind spots do not inadvertently impede progress. Facilitators must be active at the right times to handle the emotional moments that occur in many, if not most, meetings. The following competencies are required for an effective facilitator or consultant.

Neutrality

Neutrality is not taking sides when helping two parties or workgroups through issues, even if you agree more with one or the other. Facilitators must use their neutral third-party status as the need arises. Once a facilitator takes a side, they are emotionally part of the group for which they chose to be "right," and their ability to help disintegrates. In the role of consultant, neutrality is critical to help a group work through their issues. To further my point, see the following from Robert P Crosby's book *Cultural Change in Organizations.*

- Neutral about the issues. A facilitator can best be neutral when coming from a "not-knowing" position. Not knowing the inside jargon and technical aspects of the project (or issues) heighten the facilitator's awareness of the continual need for clarity.

- Capable of asserting personal authority, both in moving the process and guiding conflict resolution.
- Clear about their role as facilitator, which includes personal clarity that they are not present to be the sponsor, nor the advocate of substantive ideas, nor the project manager. In short, this is not the facilitator's project. They should not convince others of its importance. That is the sponsor's job, especially the Sustaining Sponsors (the immediate boss of each participant).
- Clear about the problem-solving steps crucial to this activity. This includes the ability to 1) organize a large group of participants, 2) manage a multistep process to identify the critical issues blocking success, and 3) plan wisely to resolve these issues.
- Highly skilled in their ability to achieve project clarity. This is especially true in two dimensions. First, the systemic change roles as outlined by Sponsor/Agent/Target/Advocate. Second, task-component clarity as defined by SPA, clarity of the task or action, and By-Whens (completion date through dialogue).

Reciprocity

The principle of reciprocity is that *it takes two to tango*, and I am part of the reason that I am not getting what I want. Therefore, I must be willing to take ownership and do something to ensure *I change the dynamic* for the desired outcome.

Example: During survey feedback process—"Review each item and identify commitments to reciprocity. For instance, suppose you ask for more clarity about who will decide when certain issues are being discussed. Your reciprocal agreement will be to ask when you are not clear." Reciprocity is an adult/adult creator model versus a parent/child/victim model (i.e., the boss will take care of me).

Conflict Utilization

Organizations are filled with pinch points and moments of tension that, if left unresolved, can easily spiral into larger conflict. The job of the facilitator is to help the group constructively manage conflict moments.

Conflict Defined - Any moment in which I am suddenly faced with a choice of what to do is a conflict moment.

Dr. Jay Hall describes conflict as follows:

> "We say, in general, that conflict exists whenever there are important differences between people, groups, or nations which, should they persist and remain unresolved, serve to keep the parties involved apart in some way."

I broaden what Dr. Hall says to include *even minor differences*. It has been my experience that any difference between two people or groups can cause the two parties to behave in the ways they have learned how to cope with conflict over the years, especially their young years. Dr. Hall goes on to say:

> "Conflict is a natural part of the human condition, but the manner in which you respond to and manage its dynamics will help determine the success of your enterprise."

and

> ". . .conflict is neither good nor bad, right nor wrong, nor does it necessarily have any of the meanings that people ordinarily attach to it. Rather, conflict dynamics are simply a very natural part of human interaction whose 'meanings' are imposed by the parties to the particular conflict."

Conflict is core to human existence and part and parcel of all workplaces. If Appendix C: The Waterline Model is correct, then most workplaces focus in the wrong place when conflict arises and, even worse, punish those for being in the conflict itself. Each workplace is different.

Instead of seeing conflict as negative, see such moments as holding promise for real change and greater systemic alignment to transform the workplace. This can only be achieved by having the courage and conviction to actually work through the conflicts that emerge. Once healthy norms are created to manage conflict, then working differences become a norm and productive work stops being halted in the face of conflict.

This approach has two critical components. First, leaders must exercise their *generative power* (see p. 71 of *SOA*) and learn a skill set to address conflicts and avoid staying stuck in blame of a person or group. Second, the consultant or facilitator must understand their own tendencies and stay focused on the effective facilitation practices during moments of conflict that allow the organization, in the form of the immediate workgroup, to constructively work through the conflict themselves. Both components require self-work, as conflict is a core EQ pattern ingrained from our upbringing. Many want to idolize one particular conflict style as the "correct" way. Hall lists five distinct styles, all of which have positive and potentially negative outcomes. Versatility, the ability to use the appropriate style in any given moment, is crucial.

I want facilitators to understand conflict dynamics and provide groups multiple ways to work through them. Chapter 9 of *FFF* provides a model to learn about yourself in conflict. The best way to learn about individual conflict styles is through an experiential training (e.g., a T-Group or any other means of learning about yourself in tense moments). The goal is flexibility. Beyond your own unique pattern in conflict, Richard Walton created a definitive list to help others manage conflict moments. On page 92 of Chapter 8, I outlined Richard Walton's rules to illustrate how to better facilitate conflict situations. Your task is to learn and live by them if you are to facilitate any of the activities in this book.

Language, Reactivity, and the Hippocampus

"We cannot use the words 'problem solving' today."

"I do not like the word 'Cascade.'"

"Bottom-line goals are the wrong way to go."

"Do not say 'Intervention.'"

Language has limitations. All workplaces and humans develop, through experience, unique meaning, and reactivity associated with certain words that remind them of a painful event.

". . . all sounds, words, gestures, and tones are interpreted in many different ways, and our ability to communicate clearly is limited. Words intended to convey a certain message are received in different ways by different people participating in the same conversation. As you read this page, you will understand its words differently than another reader. Even seemingly descriptive words like "green" have many different meanings and interpretations. If you need more paint to finish painting your house, would you call the store and simply order more "green paint" expecting to get the same shade?

Words are also circular. Look up a word in the dictionary, and you will be guided to yet another word that helps define it. Eventually you will be guided back to your first word.

Words point in many directions. "Green" can point to certain frequencies of light in the color spectrum. It can also refer to someone who is inexperienced or suggest envy. Thus, a single word may have many meanings"(Robert P Crosby, 2006, p. 65).

As a facilitator, focus on outcomes rather than words that mean something different for you than they do to your client. *The* hippocampus *is the part of the brain where memories are stored*, both pleasant and painful. Whomever you are working with may let go of their reaction to a word through a quick conversation. If they do not, then own the problem yourself and choose a different word.

I first learned this phenomenon while helping facilitate a large planning session combining hourly and salaried employees. A condition of doing the session was to not use the words "problem solving," as they were judged negatively by many staff and hourly workers. Otherwise, the session would not have occurred. The outcomes were huge. The session led to several million in savings.

The same dynamic has happened throughout my career. Suddenly I say something that triggers a person's hippocampus and they react. My rule is to clarify for a few minutes. If it is not resolved, then use another word.

The Battle for Structure and Initiative

Carl Whitaker, MD, was a family systems therapist with a unique style of working with clients. He believed the only way to heal a family was to have all members present and allow for an engagement that was genuine and authentic where the therapist was as much of a learner as the client. Therefore, he would not attempt to be "separate" and outside the system, yet would also not pretend to initially understand them. "How could I? I just met them." Whitaker believed if he could provide the right structure and allow the client to take initiative, then a healing process would happen through an experiential, interactive process.

His experience allowed him to develop two battles for success: Battle for Structure and Battle for Initiative. I will explain each battle and then derive implications to consulting in organizations.

The Battle for Structure is the minimum conditions required to help. For Whitaker and Napier, it was the decision of who will attend the therapy meeting. Napier and Whitaker (1978) say, "Every [family] member is important," and when families "elect" to attend therapy without a particular family member, they are not only deciding to go against the therapist's request, they are also sending a subtle (or not so subtle) message to the missing member: The missing member will wonder, "Do I matter?"

Further, "Families come into therapy with their own structure, and tone, and rules. Their organization, their pattern, has been established over years of living, and it is extremely meaningful and very painful for them. They would not be in therapy if they were happy with it. But however faulty, the family counts on the familiarity and predictability of their world. If they are going to turn loose this painful predictability and attempt to reorganize themselves, they need firm external support" (Napier & Whitaker, 1978, p. 11).

"The key point here is for the therapist to face the need to act with personal and professional integrity. You must act on what you believe. Betrayals help no one. The Battle for Structure is really you coming to grips with yourself and then presenting this to them. It's not a technique or a power play. *It's a setting of the minimum conditions you require before beginning.*"

The Battle for Initiative is who owns the will to succeed and continue fighting for more effectiveness. Therefore, issues to resolve must come from the client after establishing a relationship with the therapist.

> "If therapy was to succeed, [the family] had to know, early in the process, that their initiative, their will to fight and struggle and push and try, was essential to a successful outcome." (Napier and Whitaker, 1978, p. 62).

Here are further thoughts about initiative and the therapeutic process from an interview with William Bumberry.

> **Whitaker:** ". . . I want them to be clear that I'm not artificially playing host. I'm like any surgeon. I'm interested in getting the pathology resolved, not in preventing the flow of blood. They need to know that it's painful, so they're prepared. Just like a dentist would tell you, "You know this is going to hurt" before he puts the needle in your tooth.
>
> I call this the Battle for Initiative really. It's making them maintain the initiative in their own life. It's making sure that the anxiety they came with stays there. That they don't go anxiety-free and collapse and expect me to handle their world."
>
> **Bumberry:** "But they're coming to you for some help with their anxiety. That's why they're there! You're saying you're not going to do that?"
>
> **Whitaker:** "That's right! I do not want to relieve their anxiety. I want their anxiety to be the power that makes things move. Then I want to combine with it to make their anxiety more productive."

Whitaker further states, "When a family approaches a therapist, all members want their personal views validated. While this is their desire, it is not what they need. What is needed is an experience that will free them from the blocked perspectives they have developed. They need the opportunity to see their family in a more complicated light. To shed the distorting good-vs.-bad dichotomies they have regressed to. In effect, they need to have their comfort disrupted. They need to be freed to develop the kind of anxiety required to fuel them in a massive growth effort."

Now I will apply Whitaker's two battles to improving organizations.

First the *Battle for Structure*. I believe that organizations continually search for ways to do things faster, yet they can become myopic when attempting to solve things. Quick fixes are often the norm. The pressure to have employees do their daily tasks outweighs taking the time for well-structured dialogue to address issues that hurt productivity. *Making sure the right people are in the right conversations to solve problems is the battle for structure.*

Therefore, if solving a problem on the floor, I must include the people that work on the floor in some significant way to ensure the right issues are raised and the right solutions are implemented. Structures related to the Battle for Structure in the workplace are as follows:

- Structure to follow during meeting.
- Are the Targets (see *SOA*, Chapter 9, Worker Knowledge) involved in the improvements (i.e., they helped shape, test, implement, and raise issues)?
- Is there clear Sponsorship, Decision Making, Governance?
- Correct sequence of process steps.
- The right amount in groups when managing a large process.

Now the *Battle for Initiative*. When leading a well-structured session, are the participants raising and addressing the issues collectively, or are you doing most of the talking and raising the issues to solve? The Battle for Initiative involves, after achieving a solid structure, allowing the topics, issues, and energy to improve to *flow from the employees*, including the following:

- What issues get raised.
- Allow long pauses of silence until an issue is raised.
- Gate keeping (inviting someone to talk) when a person that should talk does not talk.
- Focus the employees to talk directly to each other.
- Help face rather than avoid conflict.
- Allow space for those in conflict to talk directly.

A conscious awareness of the battles for structure and initiative and living within your own boundaries helps the consultant better serve their client in solving their own problems and increasing their own capabilities.

Facilitator Theory Competencies (and Sources)

Beyond neutrality, reciprocity, conflict utilization, and the battles for structure and initiative, there are many theories to learn and use at any given moment. Presented here is a list to help you become more proficient in your craft. I am not saying these are the only needed or useful theories. However, they are the core theories to aid your abilities as a successful consultant or facilitator.

I also expect a high level of competency. To help explain competency, I created the following learning levels.

Level I—I understand the basics of the theory.

Level II—I can give the theory.

Level III—I can source the theory ad hoc without notes.

Level IV—I can be the theory.

As a facilitator or consultant intending to successfully use the activities in this book, you must develop at least a Level II understanding of each theory while *striving* to operate at Level IV. This is especially important, and perhaps most difficult, if you are internal to your workplace and have developed close relationships with peers and members within your own work team (the fusion state of herding and silos go hand in hand, see Chapter 4 of *Leadership Can Be Learned*). Therefore, if you are protective of your group rather than rising above the individual to the whole system, then you are by definition in a fused moment, have lost your ability to be neutral, and therefore, are not in your facilitator role. I expect that to happen because we, after all, are all human. The trick is to identify it, treat yourself with grace, and then intervene to increase whole system health.

My expectation is that you strive toward Level IV competency in each of the following theories.

- **Decision Making** (Chapters 12 and 13 of *SOA*; Appendix E: Delegation of CCIO)
- **The Interpersonal Gap** (Chapters 3 and 4 of *FFF*)
- **The Four Key Skills** (Chapter 4 of *FFF*, especially Behavioral Specifics)
- **Victim/Creator** (Appendix B)
- **SOCIAL STYLE** (Appendix A)
- **VLOMP** (Chapter 8, p. 98)

- **Sponsor Agent Target Advocate** (Chapters 3, 5, 6, and 11 of *SOA*)
- **Self-Differentiated Leadership** (*Leadership Can Be Learned,* especially Chapter 15)
- **Systems Thinking** (see *SOA,* plus a variety of family systems thinkers such as Edwin Friedman, Murray Bowen, Carl Whitaker, and Salvador Minuchin)
- **Accountability and Follow-up** (Chapters 7 and 10 of *SOA*)

Conclusion

By using the principles in this and the following chapter, I am confident that you will lead the activities in this book to a level that will add value to any group. Apply the principles outlined by these theories and you will succeed as a facilitator, even if you are not perfect. After reaching Level III awareness of the theories, you can apply the third-party conflict skills, ad hoc, at any time even if a formal session is not created.

CHAPTER 8

The Facilitator Triangle

"Perhaps the greatest of all pedagogical fallacies is the notion that a person learns only the particular thing they are studying at the time."
—John Dewey

Introduction

Healthy engagement is accelerated when employees learn how to be direct with each other in appropriate ways. This chapter teaches how to facilitate such interactions. You can model and teach these skills in each meeting, event, or impromptu moment at work. In fact, whether you realize it or not, you are already teaching how to be direct or indirect by your actions and behaviors. John Dewey called such indirect teachings "collateral learning." Teacher–students interactions, conscious or not, set an expectation that shapes future interactions.

One can learn to be conscious of such moments and build their capability to help the organization move toward greater functioning, better engagement, and, ultimately, higher productivity.

The following discussion will help employees be more direct in any situation. This information is especially important in moments of conflict or tension. Therefore, this chapter uses as its frame conflict management between employees. Make no mistake: what you are about to learn is vital to ensure the work happens between the right people and that you improve your facilitation skills in any situation.

This chapter complements Chapters 5, 6, and 7 related to conflict. The goal is to provide a more complete picture of the nuts and bolts of facilitating a third-party conflict session. Third-party means you are facilitating two or more people through a conflict of which you are not personally involved. This chapter specifically focuses on the behaviors needed by the facilitator when working with two people in conflict. These same behaviors are needed to effectively facilitate any group of people and are often absent, allowing the participants to miss key learnings.

If third-party conflict is done well, the participants learn how to manage the conflict by doing the skills needed to be successful. A skilled facilitator ensures that each participant learns by using a *behavioral science model* to work through the current conflict and build their capacity to successfully navigate future conflicts (see Figure 16). Third-party conflict management as taught in this book stays true to applied behavioral science and allows for maximum ownership of all parties.

In contrast, conflict management using a different and more common *popular conflict model* builds a dependent relationship with the facilitator (see Figure 15). The popular conflict model ensures future conflicts are brought to the facilitator, who remains in the expert role by deciding who is right or wrong. In the popular conflict model, the facilitator uses skills that could be taught and used by the participants, such as paraphrase, and miss the opportunity to transfer those skills to the participants. Thus, the culture remains stuck in a more dysfunctional pattern. This model is primarily used because facilitators have not been taught another way.

The popular conflict model allows morale issues to linger as participants are less likely to take ownership and understand their part of the conflict by playing a more passive role in its management. They miss the opportunity conflict allows to build the skills needed to work through future conflicts and learn about self.

The following list of third-party facilitator qualities is core when using the applied behavioral science model and it is adapted from *Managing Conflict: Interpersonal Dialogue and Third-Party Roles*, by Richard E. Walton.

1. High expertise in process work.
2. Low power over the fate of participants.
3. High control over process.
4. Moderate knowledge of issues involved.
5. Third-party neutrality.

This chapter focuses on number 3, high control over process. A few components of the process are key to ensure effective conflict management and that participants are better equipped to manage future conflicts. I will focus on the mechanics of conducting the in-action portion of third-party conflict and two behavioral components.

Behavioral Components

The facilitator must be highly skilled in using and recognizing paraphrase, parrot, perception check, feeling description, and behavioral description. These skills are required to teach and coach the participants to work through their conflict.

The skills sound simple but are not easy, especially in tense situations when you need them most. Here is a quick refresher of each skill.

- **Behavioral Description:** Describing behavior without judgment/interpretation
- **Feeling Description:** Describe one's own feeling
- **Perception Check:** Check/guess the feeling of another
- **Paraphrase:** Explore meaning of another's statement
- **Parrot:** Repeat another's exact words

For an in-depth understanding of each skill, read Chapter 4 of *Fight, Flight, Freeze*, by Gilmore Crosby. *Our belief is that if you cannot live these skills in tense moments, then you are not capable of third-party facilitation.*

Beyond those core skills is the ability to self-differentiate. This ability is critical to move beyond "fusion" to honoring what others say as truth of themselves. In other words, if Person A says, "This is what I think," and Person B says, "No it is not; you think this," then Person B is fused. Meaning, Person B believes to know more about Person A than Person A. A facilitator's job is to help encourage, guide, and shift participants toward honoring the other's word.

People often say things in tense moments, and then others try to hold them to what *they are sure* they heard. In reality, the ability to know exactly what was said even five minutes earlier in a calm state is very difficult. Add tension and that ability significantly decreases. Therefore, *arguing about what was said is a futile endeavor.* All one can do is learn from each moment, as best one can, and then commit toward improving the working relationship now and into the future.

Effective third-party conflict management requires understanding the emotional process of venting. All people vent, yet they do so in their own unique way. A common conflict is to fight over vents. I call this venting about venting. This happens when one thinks that my way of venting is better than yours. Here are some common vents about venting.

"Can you believe she stormed out of that meeting?"

"He is screaming and yelling again!"

"I hate it when she gets quiet and says nothing!"

"Don't raise your voice at me!"

While this is not a chapter about venting, it is helpful to understand the different venting styles that can be derived from Merrill and Reid's four SOCIAL STYLEs: Driving Style, Analytical Style, Expressive Style, and Amiable Style (see Appendix A). SOCIAL STYLE is a model of behavior that highlights diversity at work in the form of different operating styles. In reality, peoples' venting patterns were likely shaped years ago and are much harder to change than clearing up issues in conflict. Skilled facilitators recognize this dynamic and can quickly help people move beyond arguments about how each other vents.

I am not advocating that all venting should be tolerated in organizations. Rather, I am advocating for an understanding of the emotional process of venting and learning how to use it productively. If you do not understand the emotional process of venting and set norms about behaviors in your organization, then those norms will most likely reflect the prevailing SOCIAL STYLE that is accepted and, therefore, punish that type's shadow side (i.e., that side of yourself that you are troubled with and therefore see as "bad," or "inappropriate"). If the norms in your business tend toward the Analytical Style, then beware if you tend toward the Expressive Style. If the norm tends toward the Driving Style, then beware if you tend toward the Amiable Style. If the norm is the Expressive Style, then beware if you tend toward the Analytical Style, and so on.

When facilitating third parties, focus on the five core behavioral skills. Also, coach each participant to honor the *here and now* words of the other and let go of past beliefs of what they think the other said or meant. *The parties in conflict should experience a journey of discovery and learning about self while honoring the other.* Core behavioral science skills, especially behavioral description and active listening (paraphrase and parrot), are key to that discovery.

The popular conflict model and behavioral science model will further illustrate this topic. Then I will review the key mechanics necessary to effectively lead third party, be it formal or ad hoc, using the behavioral science model.

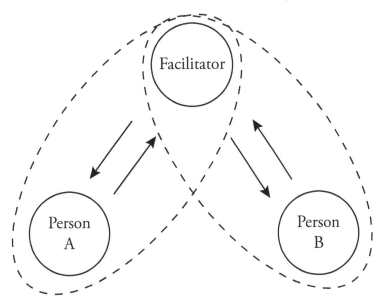

Figure 15 Popular Conflict Model

Popular Conflict Model - The facilitator assumes the "expert role" and listens to both sides of the story, determines who is right or wrong (or some combination), and then tells the participants their decision of how to resolve the differences.

This model is useful occasionally if people truly cannot work through conflicts (also important in society when people or organizations need legal* help). This model fails when managing workplace conflict, especially if it is the primary method. It creates dependence on the expert facilitator, hurts or inhibits participant learning, invites pop psychology, and does not teach how to solve future issues. Therefore, the participants have a greater likelihood of exiting the conflict blaming the other, not learning or owning their part, and/or building dependence on the expert to solve future problems.

The popular conflict model does not have to be trained. Rather, it must be brought into awareness. It is how most learned to behave through the socialization process. As children we are taught to blame and point fingers, so most, if not all, have the tendency to assign blame and take sides in the midst of conflict. Unless the facilitator is trained on the mechanics of third party using the behavioral science model, and is aware of and can come from a place of neutrality, they will almost surely slip into the popular conflict model of resolving conflict. Therefore, the parties involved in the conflict are let "off the hook" to manage the issue and, most importantly, learn about themselves in the process.

There are times in organizations, however, when systemic issues are discovered that must be decided by the proper authority. Those in the role of boss, when they see their employees in conflict, must think systemically and solve those issues. They include being unclear about SATA, priorities, roles, goals, assignments, and decision making (see Appendix C: The Waterline Model). The skilled facilitator listens for such items while conducting third-party conflict sessions and helps participants bring the right issues to the right people to solve. Beyond systemic issues, most likely the parties in conflict have had a series of misunderstandings and likely have different operating styles (see Appendix A: SOCIAL STYLE). To learn about oneself in a conflict, one must have the ability to truly listen to as much clean feedback as possible by using the skills outlined on the previous page. The behavioral science model starts with the assumption that the participants have this capability (almost all people do).

The path to enable this is the behavioral science model.

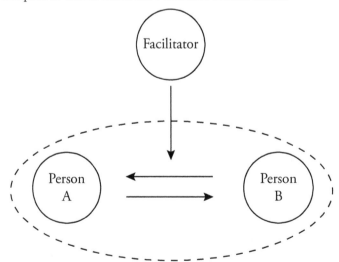

Figure 16 Behavioral Science Model

Behavioral Science Model - The facilitator helps the participants in conflict talk to each other using the aforementioned behavioral skills. This transfers to future interactions and increases the odds of resolving their own conflicts. By using this model, the participants have a greater chance to learn and understand each other and themselves.

Facilitators must understand and differentiate between the two models to ensure they don't slide toward the popular conflict model, which is the prevailing norm in most organizations. Even if the facilitator intends to use the behavioral model, *it is easy to start paraphrasing each participant rather than have them paraphrase each other.* This subtle shift to the popular conflict model happens when the facilitator judges, rightly or wrongly, that the participants cannot do the work.

If the facilitator paraphrases each participant, instead of having the people working through the conflict paraphrase each other, then they have slipped into the popular conflict model. Consequently, those in conflict are "off the hook" because they don't have to actively listen to each other. Occasionally, it is appropriate as a facilitator to say what you think a person in the conflict is saying, if one party is struggling to accurately paraphrase the other. I call that *alter ego.* However, once you slip into the popular conflict model and start doing behaviors that the participants themselves should be doing, you hurt the participants' ability to learn because they are not doing the skills.

Alter ego means speaking for one of the participants as if I am that person. I use it *as a last resort* to help paraphrase when the person has given a few attempts and is obviously not able to convey what the other just said. Stick with the behavioral model first by giving your expectations, inviting them to convey what the other said, and if they cannot, then alter ego to get beyond the immediate stuck moment. However, when you alter ego, be clear that you are attempting to speak as if you are the person in the conflict whom you want to understand what the other is saying. Therefore, move directly behind the person you are helping (alter ego-ing). Only do so after receiving permission to be them for a moment. The goal is to teach paraphrase by modeling it temporarily.

I will now illustrate the facilitator role in the various steps of a third-party conflict. To do so I reference Chapter 5, Employee–Employee Conflict. Section three focuses on the meeting where the parties work through their conflict. The first stage of a formal process includes meeting with and preparing each participant to work through the conflict. Preparation includes listening to their issues, teaching and coaching core behavioral skills, overviewing the meeting, and getting a commitment to raise the tough issues.

VLOMP

The third-party conflict-management process flows in the following way, using a model called VLOMP by Robert P Crosby. It is essential to 1) follow a conceptual conflict-management process, 2) use the behavioral skills listed on p. 93, and 3) follow the behavioral science models in Figures 17, 18, and 19. The particular conceptual model does not matter as much as ensuring 2 and 3.

Here is the VLOMP conceptual conflict-management process.

Ventilation: Allow the individuals to share their frustrations. Empathy from you, the third party, without taking sides is the required skill. Hopefully, prepared by the interview, the parties are ready to "vent" using minimal blame.

Listen: While the first person is venting, the other participant must listen and repeat what the person said. No arguing or defending is allowed. John Wallen states that most conflict happens from misunderstanding the meaning intended by the other. Parroting (or a loose version of it) is one way to ensure people actually hear what the other said versus fighting against it. Forcing listening slows the conversation and lessens the intensity. Often when participants parrot accurately, they hear the other for the first time. Almost always it will shift the conflict in a positive direction.

Openness: Participants must be open to reflect on their part of the conflict and emotional reaction to events. Help the individuals move from venting to sharing responsibility for the problem. The components of openness include describing feelings about specific behaviors (by either participants) and each individual being open to learn about how they co-created the conflict. Owning is about describing one's part in the co-creation. Owning is not about taking complete responsibility for the conflict (i.e., letting the other off the hook) nor making excuses by telling a story about your past (appropriately owning eases tension yet may more easily follow the Moccasin step).

Moccasin: Help each party walk in the other's moccasins, to understand where the other person is coming from and be able to say, "I can see how you could have felt or acted that way." Paraphrase and hunch the other's emotion, communicating that you are "getting it."

Plan for change:
- Provide specific examples of the problem.
- Be specific with requests for change.
- Make sure the requested changes are measurable. (A note about what is measurable: Many don't want to write down behavioral items but they must be tracked. Things such as, "If I think you are ignoring a request from me, I will ask." This can be tracked by checking a spreadsheet.)
- Reciprocity—This means taking appropriate responsibility for my own requests. An inappropriate commitment would be, "OK, I will give you the data when you need it" (when the data is needed at inconsistent times that only the person who needs it knows) versus "If I want data I will ask" (appropriate reciprocity by the user of the data). Reciprocity helps people take appropriate responsibility to acquire what they want.

Third-Party Mechanics

Here are the steps in the behavioral science model where third-party mechanics are critical.

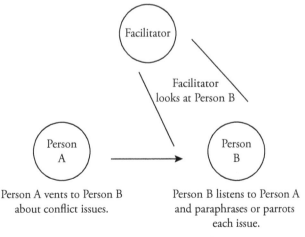

Figure 17 Facilitator Role in Vent and Listen Stage

Vent and Listen Stage Mechanics—During the vent and listen stage, either Person A or Person B starts venting. In Figure 17, Person A starts venting. The facilitator must explain that Person A is to vent and Person B is to listen. *No defending is allowed. Each participant must be fully prepped on the difference between a judgment and behavioral specific and to only share their behavioral specifics.* But even so, Person B may be tempted to start defending, or indeed may have a lifetime habit of it, so the facilitator must stop it when it starts and help them say back what they heard.

The facilitator must also recognize when *the paraphrases are not really paraphrases but fights and arguments* and stop them. Conversely, if Person A starts by saying a hard judgment, even after they have been coached to say the specifics, the facilitator must also stop it. The goal is to learn about specifics and understand each other's position and perspective.

The basic process is that Person A says their issue and then Person B paraphrases. The facilitator then asks Person A if Person B has got it right. If yes, on to the next issue. If no, stay on the current issue until Person B can accurately paraphrase until Person A agrees. Sometimes Person B says it perfect and Person A says, "No, that is not it." It is OK for the facilitator to share their surprise, but the focus is for Person A and B to listen and understand each other. The process continues until Person A shares all their issues and has been heard accurately. In other words, Person B paraphrases Person A's issues, and Person A acknowledges that Person B understands. Then you switch and follow the opposite pattern. Figure 18 illustrates the process.

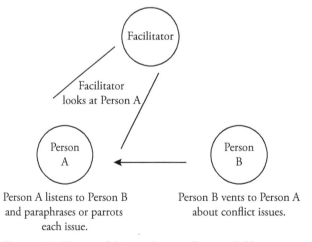

Figure 18 Vent and Listen Stage - Person B Vents

This is the same process as previously shown, yet now that Person B is venting, the facilitator must manage Person A. The other reason to do this is triangulation. The goal is to help the participants talk to each other. If, as facilitator, you look at the person talking, they have a tendency to look at you, even when talking about the other person.

All conflict sessions should focus on managing the current situation and collateral learning. That is, the way participants talk through this issue gives them the courage and skills to manage future issues, even if they are difficult. *By looking at the listener, you are helping the speaker not triangle you into the conversation and learn to be direct.*

Using your face and body to direct conversations lasts throughout the third party, especially when things get tough. In most third parties things will flow from tense to loose, to small moments of tension. The skilled facilitator navigates appropriately at each moment. These moments happen fast. Figure 19 illustrates the facilitator's actions during paraphrase moments.

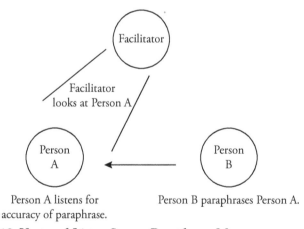

Person A listens for   Person B paraphrases Person A.
accuracy of paraphrase.

Figure 19 Vent and Listen Stage - Paraphrase Moments

Whoever is saying something to the other person, especially early in the conflict sessions, the facilitator is looking at the other person, as illustrated in Figures 17, 18, and 19.

Going forward, the facilitator can slip in and out of this strict structure and help as needed. The conversation can become more circular after completing the venting stage and quality listening starts happening consistently.

Ad Hoc Use of Method - After learning how to help people listen to each other in a formal process, *the obvious implications to meetings and other work scenarios become clear.* It is easy to find scenarios in which people are not listening to each other. The person not being heard often repeats themselves or continues in hopes to finally be understood.

Why not take a different tact? If you see someone not being heard and others arguing instead of listening, ask someone to convey what they think the other is saying. Most people cannot. Then have them keep trying until they get it. When they do paraphrase it accurately, then the tension will likely reduce immediately. *The power of being heard and acknowledged is often quite huge, whereas the opposite is quite agonizing.*

These mechanics become easy with practice. The tricky part is letting go of the popular conflict model. If you see a group arguing and believe they should stop, then you are judging their abilities to effectively listen to each other. If you instead give these mechanics a fair shake, then you may find that people are much more capable than you think.

The aim is to create a learning organization where people can use conflict moments to learn about each other, then move forward in a more integrated way. These mechanics are critical toward achieving that outcome.

*__Professional Mediation or Arbitration__ - I want to acknowledge the skill and training needed to do professional legal work. The popular conflict model references the structure used in organizations unconsciously and not professional legal services, which people some- times use in the workplace.

CHAPTER 9

The Leadership Questions

Introduction

This chapter is a series of questions reflecting on leadership. Facilitators can use this as a guide when prepping leaders for strategic activities. Leaders can use it to focus on areas to improve. Those with balance in the following list will help their organizations become even more successful.

List of Questions: Read and self-reflect on these questions. Then focus on areas of improvement.

Is your group working toward measurable goals?
- Do your goals reflect your workgroup's bottom line?
- Do you measure and track the critical processes needed to reach those goals?
- Do you regularly involve your employees to troubleshoot ways to achieve your goals?

Do you own all that happens in your work area?
- Do you also own problems that occur, in part, by the supporting resources working in your area, but over whom you have no legitimate authority (i.e., you do not do their performance review)?

- If a supporting resource is not servicing your group and should, do you blame that person instead of working with them until you get the required results?
- If your group does not receive inputs on time or meet quality standards (materials, data, money, people), do you blame those responsible or work through the issues?
- Can you catch your blame and turn it into constructive problem solving to achieve results?

How is your ability to self-differentiate as a leader? Self-differentiation is measured by your ability to show up in tense moments and own your experience by articulating it (take a stand) and honoring the other(s) by actively listening (stay connected) without adding your judgments. Losing either capability reduces your ability to differentiate yourself from the other.

- In a tense moment, can you clearly articulate what you want and convey your full experience using nonblaming language (i.e., this is what I think, this is what I feel, [mad, sad, glad, afraid], and this is what I want or prefer)?
- Can you perform the previous question, stay engaged, and fully understand and paraphrase what they want, think, and feel, regardless of their perspective?
- Is your focus mainly on the first bullet (taking stands)?
- Is your focus mainly on the second bullet (connection)?

Are you so used to problems that you just live with them? Has your advocacy backbone died?

- Do you have a problem-solving frame that begins with analysis to get to the facts of the issue or do you attempt to solve problems by quick solutions and no real analysis?

How is your workplace emotional intelligence?

- Are you aware of the connection between thoughts and feelings?
- Are you aware of the process of venting and how to tune into people that are doing it *versus* reacting against or avoiding them? Or when people vent, do you help perpetuate a cycle of venting about their vent, which adds more rifts and problems?

- Do you know the difference between a judgment of someone, such as any adjective used to describe another, and a behavioral description, which is an attempt to identify the behavioral facts of what a person did including the actual words used by that person? (Words are observable behavior. However, memory cannot be 100% trusted, so when one shares the words they thought they heard, they must understand that they are likely at least a little off.)
- Are you aware of the dynamics of triangles in the workplace? Can you help people have direct, constructive conversations rather than stay in dysfunctional triangles?

Can you engage, or are you disconnected as a leader?

- Is it clear you are the leader during a meeting with your workgroup, or do you appear as if you are one of the employees, or are you more passive than most in your workgroup?
- Do you stop conversations when obvious solutions arise or that are about things already decided, and redirect the group toward working through the next issue(s)?
- Do you confront behavior that is counterproductive to effective workplaces, like not paying attention or texting during meetings instead of listening and participating?
- When employees raise issues, can you engage by helping get to the behavioral specifics, or do you avoid the topic or complain like you are an employee rather than the leader?
- Do you confront people working outside of expectations and help them understand the actual behavioral expectations, while appropriately reprimanding those who are truly being insubordinate?
- Do you catch people doing things right and let them know by providing specific, positive reinforcement? Do you share positive feedback more than negative criticism (at least three positives to one negative)?

As a leader, do you tend to focus on the forest or in the trees? The forest represents overall functioning of the group and strategy. The trees represent tasks without looking at the whole group.

- Are you stuck in one or the other or are you flexible? If you are in the trees, can you focus sufficiently on the forest and create strategies that positively impact the group? If you look only at the forest, can you focus sufficiently on the trees and hold people accountable for individual tasks?
- No matter your tendency, can you engage your employees when they raise issues? Or do you try various means to stop them from talking, such as 1) not saying anything or 2) acting *as if* you are one of them and complain while not leading them toward a solution?

When starting new initiatives, do you stick to them and follow through until they are working well?

- Or are you in the never-ending cycle of starting things without following through to ensure success?

Do you listen to the people doing the work, such as floor personnel, and ensure they have the inputs and resources to do their job?

- Or do you try to get them to stop complaining and get to work?

Do you maintain your focus on business results and continually engage your employees to raise and resolve issues in the way of success?

- Or do you focus on keeping peace and avoiding tension? Do you see dissenters as troublemakers?
- Or do you attempt to understand each complaint to its behavioral facts and then implement solutions to solve issues as needed?

How is your balance between backbone (overtly decisive, confront appropriately, make decisions, and hold people accountable), heart (tune in, express empathy, listen deeply in tense moments, and convey that you care), head (provide vision, think through difficult problems, help people understand role and expectations, and connect to the current situation), and guts (trust your instincts and speak your truth using nonblaming language in difficult moments)?

- Where are you stuck and deficient in these dimensions?

Interactive Skills - How would you rate your interactive skills? (See Figure 20.) Beyond legitimate authority, interacting successfully with your employees is one of the most important ways to develop effective work relationships with your team. If Gallup is right, the relationship between boss and employees is critical to create an engagement culture. Your interactive skills are extremely important to improve your work relations.

Interactive Skill Scale

	Stage	Description of Level	Inner Beliefs and Perceptions of Reality
	+6	Empathic connection with others, yet still decisive	"I can walk in your moccasins and be myself, which includes being decisive."
High	+5	Is clear about wants	"I'll tell you what I need to succeed."
	+4	Acknowledgement of one's own part in the interaction	"I help create the dance."
	+3	Nonblaming; is specific about behavior and emotions	"Telling it straight is to give noninterpretive feedback."
Med	+2	Blaming, but is behaviorally specific	"Naming your behaviors proves my judgement."
	+1	Inner awareness, but manifest in blaming	"My judgements are the truth about you."
	0	Inner awareness, but noncommunicative	"If I stay quiet, things will be 'cool'."
Low	-1	Inner awareness, but outward distortion	"Telling the truth will make it worse."
	-2	Unaware, with 'cool' blaming	"Let reason conquer emotions."

Figure 20 Interactive Skill Scale

Conclusion

Whether you are a leader or facilitator, use this list to sharpen and broaden your skills. Facilitators can use the list to 1) broaden their capabilities and 2) prepare the leader you are working with for the strategic activity. To do the latter, think about the leader you will be working with and pick one or two areas to discuss before the session. Leaders should read and reflect on areas to improve their leadership balance.

The list provided is not all inclusive. Yet, it provides a reflective tool to enhance yourself no matter your role.

APPENDIX A

Social Style®

Perhaps the greatest unconscious diversity in most organizations has nothing to do with race or any other "ism" and is more related to operating Styles of the employees.

This appendix is an adaptation of a theory called SOCIAL STYLE, first created by David Merrill and Roger Reid. SOCIAL STYLE is a practical and simple way to explore how one interacts with another. The theory frames different operating Styles as a potentially huge diversity issue within organizations. It can be given alone, but it is most powerful as an add-on to another activity. It is incredibly useful when working with intact work teams, especially the ones that have been working together for a while.

This version is slightly adapted from Merrill and Reid and represents the depth I give when presenting the theory. SOCIAL STYLE is practical and intuitive. For a more in-depth version of the theory and to take an online assessment, go to www.tracomcorp.com*.

SOCIAL STYLE provides a simple way to help employees understand the diversity of operating Styles that exist within all workplaces. It helps 1) provide a simple way to understand self, 2) teach how to work better with others who operate in different Styles, and 3) provide a systemic snapshot of any work team and, by doing so, often highlights components that need addressing to improve productivity.

After understanding your position in the four-box model, you can see patterns of tension with others who are in a different place or, potentially, power struggles with those that are similar.

I generally believe less is better, so I present a simple version of SOCIAL STYLE that, for the most part, employees are able to understand quickly.

What follows is the sequence I use to give the theory, including how to present each section.

Step-by-Step Instructions

Step 1—Introduce Theory. Facilitator says, "SOCIAL STYLE is a four-box model created by David Merrill and Roger Reid. I like it because it is a simple way to do three things."

- Learn about **self**
- Learn how to work with **others**
- Learn about **systemic** implications of the group (I normally write the bold words on a flip chart.)

Step 2—Continuums. Have the participants line up on two continuums in the room. Use the following sequence and instructions.

Continuum 1 "To do this I need you all to stand up." Have them stand up and face you in the back of a large open space.

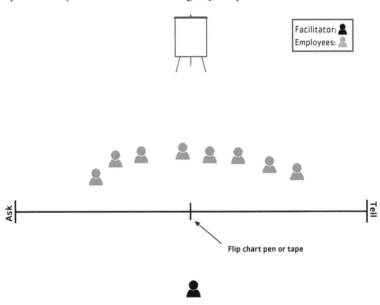

Room must be approximately 12 ft by 12 ft

Figure 21 Starting Spot for Continuums

Figure 21 illustrates where the facilitator stands in relationship to the flip chart, which is critical when giving this theory. Follow Figure 21 exactly so the participants can easily read the chart when you present the theory. The chart placement represents the model spatially.

Then say, "I want you to think about how you respond in a moment of slight tension. Do you tend to ask questions or be quiet? If so, you belong to this side of the continuum (point to the Ask side). Or do you tend to tell people what to do? If so, you belong on this side of the continuum (point to the Tell side)." Describe the continuum further by saying, "The extreme is 100% Ask. Halfway between the extreme Ask and the middle is 75% Ask and 25% Tell. The middle is 50/50. Then halfway between the middle and the extreme of Tell is 25% Ask and 75% Tell, and, finally, 100% Tell. Think about where you would place yourself on the continuum and go to that place on the line . . . now. The only place you cannot stand is 50/50 (hence the pen or tape)."

After the employees move to their locations say, "OK, in the original assessment by Merrill and Reid, you completed the questionnaire on yourself, then had five other people complete it on you. We will do this by only asking two questions, yet your opinions about each other are important. In fact, their original research found that we often see ourselves differently than others. Therefore, who would be willing to step out from the line and move people to where you think they should be?"

Sometimes the group hesitates but often people emerge. The most typical pattern is that the people from the *Tell* side of the continuum step out first. If this pattern emerges, then wait for a few of them to step out and then point it out. Also use this moment to invite the people standing in the *Ask* side to give their opinions. Whoever steps out gets to move people without debate. Here is the frame: "This is *X*'s view of the universe so your job is to move, not debate. This is only feedback, so move anywhere they want you to go."

When people are done moving, others say, "OK, now you have two choices. First, if your current spot seems right, then stay. Second, if you want to move then average out where you started and where the various people have moved you. Move to that place or stay. Now."

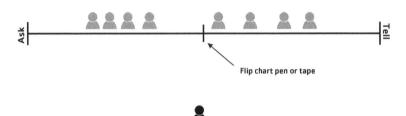

Figure 22 Continuum 1 Completed

Figure 22 represents a group that completed continuum 1. Now it is time for continuum 2.

Continuum 2—present the second continuum. "This continuum is about emotions. It is not about whether you have emotions, but whether or not you wear emotions on your sleeve. In other words, are you *transparent or not* when you feel sad, glad, mad, or afraid?"

At this point I teach the following about emotionality.

We live in an exciting time for understanding the brain. During the past 25 years, neuroscientists have begun to unlock its mysteries and reveal some of its underpinnings. Among those understandings are a multitude of ways to keep your brain healthy by continuing to develop it throughout your life. Yes, that is right! Throughout!

When I was being raised, many people thought that your brain and its embedded behavioral patterns were fully developed by age 5. We now know that is not true. In fact, the initial development of the brain is complete around the age of 25. However, the brain keeps developing throughout your life!

We either help or hinder brain development at all times. All learning, no matter how small, creates new neuropathways in the brain. By reading a book, watching educational shows, learning anything new (golf, language, craft, directions, interpersonal skills, technical skills, etc.) you help your brain. Conversely, drug or alcohol abuse, abusive relationships, car accidents, bad sleeping habits, unhealthy diets, and so on damage your brain.

We also now know that emotions truly drive your behavior. In our larger EQ Leadership training we help people understand and focus on their emotions to better control their behavior, especially in tense moments. It is exactly those moments when skills are needed to slow down and allow your neocortex to help choose your behavior wisely, rather than react in predictable patterns.

Neuroscience tells us that the limbic region of the brain, which is the seat of your emotions, has 100 neurons headed to your neocortex versus one headed from the neocortex to the limbic. Plus, that one is one fourth of the size. Your emotions drive your behavior, period. So why fight it? Instead try and understand yourself as best you can and learn how to *feel what you feel yet choose what you do.*

By understanding your brain, you can train yourself to increase your ability to see, catch, and manage your behavior during the difficult moments of your life.

"To move on this continuum, you must stay where you are in terms of the Ask/Tell continuum and move up and down the continuum of control/emote (see Figure 23)."

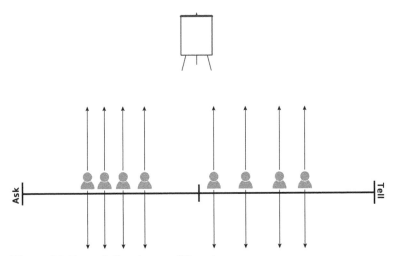

Figure 23 Second Continuum Direction

I walk to the control side of the continuum and demonstrate happiness as if "Spock" from *Star Trek* would act it out. In other words, in a *monotone* voice and *flat* face I say, "I am so happy; can't you tell how happy I am." Then I walk to the emote side and demonstrate by saying, "I am so happy; can't you tell how happy I am?" while being loud and jumping around. Then say, "However, it is not just about happiness, but rather the full range of emotions, including mad, sad, glad, and afraid. Think about where you would place yourself on the line and go there. . .now."

After the participants place themselves on the continuum, use the group to make adjustments. The rules for this stage are "Look around and see where people placed themselves and, if you think they should stand in a different spot, then suggest moving them up or down the continuum. This time I will decide using majority vote by a show of hands. If the attempt to move the person is voted down, then I will allow for one, maybe two counter suggestions that must also be decided using majority vote."

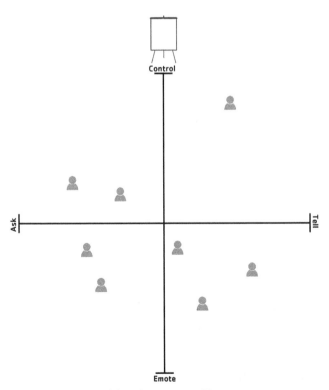

Figure 24 Participants After Continuum Two

I believe that transparency of emotions is easier to determine than the Ask-Tell continuum. Therefore, based on the group experience to this point, I may also mention my surprise about where people are standing, even if I've had a limited amount of time with them. However, I always allow majority vote to determine their final location. Usually by now more than 50% of the employees have been moved. In fact, research from The TRACOM Group shows that more than 50% of people see their SOCIAL STYLE differently than others.

When voting is done, the workgroup is now standing where they belong on the SOCIAL STYLE Model™ (see Figure 24).

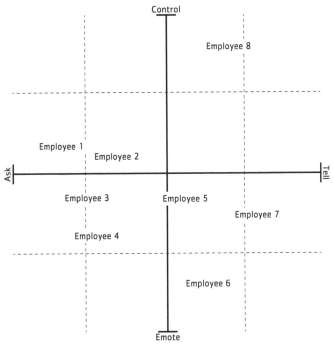

Figure 25 Participants Names on Blank Flip Chart

Write each person's name on a flip chart based on where they ended up on the chart (see Figure 25; I omitted names in this example). I tell the participants to get a chair and sit where they ended up on the model.

Step 3—Present Theory. Three things are in play right now: 1) the participants are situated where they ended up on the model, 2) each participant's name is on a flip chart for all to see, and 3) there is a blank flip chart that I use to build the theory as presented in Figure 26.

The following is how I present the theory.

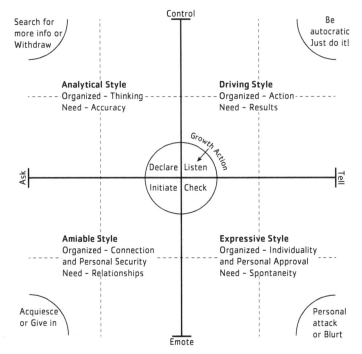

Figure 26 SOCIAL STYLE Theory Chart

"SOCIAL STYLE is a four-box model. Each box of the model is transposed to a primary and secondary Style. The upper-right corner is the *Driving Style*. The Driving Style is organized around action and their need is for results.

Each box has a *reactive state* and a *growth action*. In other words, when you react unconsciously within your primary Style, you will default to your typical reactive state. In unconscious state, the *Driving Style* will *be autocratic or start telling people what to do*. However, if you can catch yourself, then you gain the ability to learn. For the *Driving Style,* the *growth action* is to *listen.* For instance, they may say, 'Wait, hold on, would you repeat what you said so I can paraphrase to ensure my understanding.'

Once you build the discipline to do your growth action, then you gain access to all quadrants and significantly increase your versatility. *Versatility of operating Styles*, rather than being stuck in one or the other, *is key to success.*

The upper-left quadrant is the **Analytical Style**. The Analytical Style is organized around thinking, and their need is for accuracy. When in a reactive state, the Analytical Style searches for more data or withdraws.

For instance, when asked for an opinion, they might say, 'I am not sure; what if we conduct a study for six months and then compile the data to determine the best path?' It is no surprise that the Analytical Style's *growth action* is to *declare* an opinion without all the data. Growth may sound like 'I am not sure, and I would rather gather more data, but based on what I know now, I suggest *X*.'

The **Amiable Style** is organized around connection and their need is to maintain relationships. Their reactive state is to give in or acquiesce (to save the relationship of course). Their *growth action* is to *initiate* issues and concerns (Even though you may not like me, but I hope you still do!). Finally, the **Expressive Style** is organized around individuality and their need is for spontaneity. In a reactive state, the Expressive Style tends to blurt what is on their mind. Therefore, their *growth action* is to *check* the details.

All quadrants are critical for organizations. From the Analytical Style comes planning, the Driving Style is follow through and accountability, the Amiable Style holds the key to healthy work relationships, and the Expressive Style provides innovation and creativity.

Systemic Application

SOCIAL STYLE Quadrant		Organization Need
Analytical Style	⟶	Planning
Amiable Style	⟶	Work Relationships
Expressive Style	⟶	New Ideas/Creativity
Driving Style	⟶	Follow Through

Figure 27 Systemic Application of Each Quadrant

Tension with other operating Styles tends to come in one or two areas. First and most typical is the opposite quadrants. To say it a little extreme and pejoratively, the Driving Style struggles with the Amiable Style because they are social and don't get work done; the Amiable Style struggles with the Driving Style because they do not care about people. The Expressive Style struggles with the Analytical Style because they go on and on in a monotone voice and do not state an opinion; the Analytical Style struggles with the Expressive Style because they are unpredictable. The second area is the potential of power struggles with people in the same quadrant. Two Driving Styles could push in different directions, two Analytical Styles could debate facts, two Expressive Styles could argue over different creative ideas, and two Amiable Styles could differ on how people should get treated."

Dialogue—tell the group to, "Turn and talk to the person next to you about what you are *learning*. Does it seem to *fit or not fit*, and *what sense are you making of it for yourself*?" After a few minutes, field comments or questions.

Step 4—Wrap Up. I finish theory by making some final points, which are often discussed during the dialogue portion. If they are not, I make sure they are addressed.

First, I remind people that any assessment is intended to help them learn about themselves and is *not* a definition *of* them! Awareness of the Styles helps us interact and have grace for others who are different; thank goodness there are differences or life would be less meaningful. Most important is that *all Styles are critical for success and no Style is good nor bad, right nor wrong*. They simply exist and can drive behavior if you are not conscious of them. I then remind the people that movement toward versatility during tense moments is the key to success.

Second, I talk about working with each Style. Normally I do so by saying, "Merrill and Reid think that connection and effective working relationships are critical. Therefore, they believe in 'positive manipulation'. In other words, in what way should one interact when working with a Driving Style, an Amiable Style, an Analytical Style, or an Expressive Style to have an effective working relationship? How would you answer that? Imagine you are talking to four different bosses, each coming from a different quadrant. Start with the Driving Style. What do you think they would want to hear?"

I generally give the group time to answer. If they cannot, then I provide the answer. Normally many start guessing and are pretty accurate. If they do not guess, then I say the following:

- **Driving Style**—give them a bullet list of outcomes and be ready if they want to learn more details. Many in the Driving Style will not need, or at least not want, to learn more.
- **Analytical Style**—have a detailed list starting from *A* and going to *Z* about what you did, why and how, and be ready to spend ample time explaining each detail. Be ready with a bullet list of outcomes in case they want to hear them.
- **Amiable Style**—ask how they are doing and be ready to talk about either personal things such as family or about the impact the item

you are working on is having on the people, including how they are adapting to it. Be prepared to discuss personal things and only a little about actual work. However, when you finally talk about work issues, they may be resolved quickly and efficiently.

- **Expressive Style**—be prepared for a dynamic, free-flowing conversation of many ideas and topics going in multiple directions.

Third, the further you are from the middle, the more predictable your behavior. However, you are more likely to resort to your reactive mode. Conversely, the closer you are to the middle, the more versatility you have to use all SOCIAL STYLEs. That means you are also more unpredictable at any given moment.

Fourth, people tend to judge from their primary Style. Tension is often a result of others using a different operating Style from yours—likely the opposite of your Style or what a gestalt therapist may call your shadow side. This dynamic also happens within groups. The SOCIAL STYLE chart in Figure 24 only has one person in the Driving Style. That person is likely having difficulty in the group, as the predominant norm would be to show up softer and in a nondirective way.

Fifth, I always conduct a systemic analysis by reviewing how the chart unfolded. I then highlight the potential problems that a lack of awareness of the different SOCIAL STYLEs could create within the work team. The example in Figure 24 shows the dominant cultural norms of the workgroup are likely formed by the amount of Amiable Styles, Expressive Styles, and Analytical Styles. Meaning, they could get along well, generate many ideas, and yet have difficulty completing anything, especially if the one Driving Style is not the boss.

I worked with a lead team of an extrusion plant. An older machine was producing 50% of their scrap. During the discussion I said, "It seems like you have enough data to replace this machine." Then someone said, "I suggest we conduct a six-month study to determine the ways in which it is producing scrap." I referenced the newly created SOCIAL STYLE chart and said, "According to the chart, you will talk about this forever and never make the difficult decision to replace the machine" (see Figure 28).

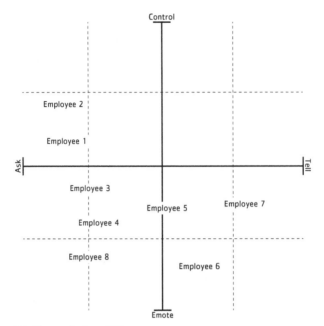

Figure 28 Example Lead Team

Once I made my point and the group took another look at the SO-CIAL STYLE systemic chart, the plant manager, who was an Amiable Style on the chart, said, "Wow, I am going to put in an RFA for the new machine first thing tomorrow." *Whatever quadrant is missing on the systemic chart you can, with predictable accuracy, help the workgroup flush out something happening that they were playing out unconsciously.* In this case it was not making decisions despite having overwhelming evidence. SO-CIAL STYLE is a powerful mental model when used right to help groups reflect and build their capacity to honor all Styles.

Conclusion

SOCIAL STYLE is a powerful way to help a group reflect on its internal dynamics. This appendix outlines what I teach in about 45 minutes. It is perhaps my most used add-on to any agenda and often yields results.

*SOCIAL STYLE content is used with permission from The TRA-COM Group. David Merrill and Roger Reid are the original founders of the TRACOM Group. SOCIAL STYLE and The Creator of SOCIAL STYLE are registered trademarks of the TRACOM Group. To learn about SOCIAL STYLE certification options, go to www.tracomcorp.com.

APPENDIX B

Victim/Creator

I create my reality. Really?

Emotional intelligence, at its core, highlights my ability to make a *distinction between seeing myself as a victim* to what just happened and, therefore, only able to blame others. Or am I able to *see myself, at least, as a cocreator* and, therefore, able to *own my part of any situation*?

Victim/Creator* is a profound and simple way to help a group claim its power and work toward greater ownership in pursuit of its goals.

What follows is how I present the theory.

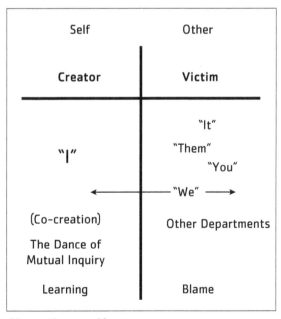

Figure 29 Victim/Creator Chart

Presenting the Theory—I present Victim/Creator as either part of a group activity or at the start of a weeklong T-Group experience.

I usually teach it in the context of how to build an accountability culture (see *SOA*, Chapter 7, Accountability). I use the following sequence to give the theory and present each stage.

Start with a blank flip chart or only have the phrase "Single Point of Accountability" and "By-When" written on the flip chart.

Have the participants sit in *pairs*, and then teach a thumbnail of SPA and By-When.

Give the theory of SPA (see SOA, Chapter 7). Have participants rate SPA by saying, "Think about the people you work with in your organizations and rate how well SPA is working on *a scale of 1 to 10*, 10 being high. If you rate SPA a 10, then for each task, role, or action you know exactly who to call to check status. If you rate SPA a 1, then you have no clue.

Please write one number on your piece of paper (either have them write on a notepad or create a small anonymous survey as outlined on page 33). Everybody has one number on their piece of paper? Good."

Give theory of By-Whens (see *SOA*, Chapter 7). Have participants rate By-Whens by saying, "Think about the people you work with in your organizations and rate how well By-Whens are working on a scale of 1 to 10, 10 being high. If it is a 10, then you will know when each task or action will be completed, and those dates are 80% accurate. You are told about the remaining 20% before they are late, which allows you to organize interconnected tasks that would have slipped on their completion dates had you not known. Most actions are dependent on other tasks. Therefore, it is critical to communicate when dates are slipping to ensure on-time completion. If dates are never set, then that is a 1. Anything in between is somewhere on the scale between 1 and 10.

Please write one number on your piece of paper (either have them write on a notepad or create a small anonymous survey as outlined on page 33). Everybody has one number on their piece of paper? Good."

At this point, either follow the guidelines to tally the data for the group to see or have participants review their own scores. Figure 30 is an actual rating from a workgroup. As you can see, they have some work to

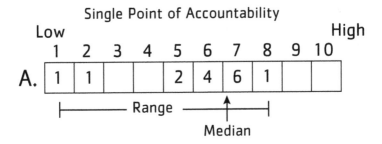

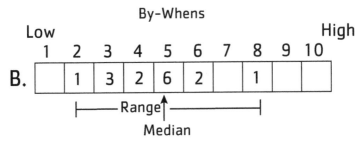

Figure 30 Example SPA and By-When Rating

do, which is common. Gathering and revealing feedback is beneficial, as it provides a baseline.

Experiential Exercise—Ask the critical question. *This question is multi-directional and must be precisely worded to the participants.* The wording allows each person to answer in either the victim or creator role. Most catch themselves in the victim role in which many, if not all, often slip into unconsciously.

Wording of Critical Question—I say, "Pick one of the two dimensions and turn and talk to your partner and answer the question, '*What would have to happen for the score to be even higher?*'" Then allow a few minutes for the participants to answer. Go to each pairing and make sure all participants speak. If one pair has not switched to the other talking, direct them to do so and give them another minute.

Next, say, "I want to use your conversation to illustrate a key EQ concept. Imagine you had an audio of what you just said to each other and could analyze that audio by looking at the actual words each of you spoke."

Now say, "I am going to claim that there was one of two ways you predominately discussed the topic."

Draw the "T" of the chart (see Figure 29).

Draw the words on the right side and add any words that are used in the culture where you are working.

Ask if anyone would be willing to admit they were talking from that side of the paper for at least some of the time.

Add the word "Victim" at the top right of the "T" (see Figure 29).

Contrast victim language by providing an example of speaking as a creator. Say something like, "You know, I am often at meetings and do not ask for By-Whens when I need them. I must change my behavior."

Add the word "I" in a large letter on the left side of the sheet. Add the word "Creator" opposite of "Victim."

Complete the remaining words while explaining each one until the chart resembles Figure 29.

Ask the participants to turn and talk to the person next to you about the following:

- What are they learning?
- Does it make sense?
- How does it relate to them?

Dialogue—When you hear the energy wane or after a few minutes say, "What came up in your conversations?" Listen and affirm what the participants say and are learning. You may also make slight corrections in their thinking.

Round Two—After the theory dialogue, have each pair redo the dialogue about how to improve the SPA or By-When score while focusing only on *creator* language. Give them a few minutes, then call cut. Ask if the conversation felt any different while talking exclusively from the creator.

The Power of "I" Language

Language holds the key to ownership of thoughts, feelings, wants, and actions. To speak from the "I" is not about selfishness but rather clarity. An effective facilitator helps a group move from the language of blame and outside-in speech to ownership and inside-out speech. Organizations moving toward greater whole system health help focus their employees to own each moment through diligence of language. It is simple yet profound and definitely not easy.

The task is to say "I" when it is "I," and "We" when it is a "We," as in we worked on this together or we talked about this and agree. The task, even more importantly, is to not say things like We think when it is really "I" think. When you nurture the "I" that shows up and encourage genuine conversations using the four key Wallen skills, then your organization can rapidly discuss difficult issues with relative ease.

"I" language removes unnecessary blame. That is, adjectives used in tense moments are almost always received as blaming. So from a blaming statement, "The warehouse was negligent," to an accurate statement, "The warehouse personnel delivered the part two hours later than I thought they would." From, "You made me mad," to "When you came in and sat down without saying anything, I felt mad."

Which statements would you rather hear? I language, which I translate to creator statements, is a key behavioral science skill needed for learning.

Conclusion

Once you help a group realize they can create what they want, within boundaries of course, then amazing things can happen. Victim/Creator is a simple way to shift energy from blame to creation.

*This theory is not intended to downplay actual victims. Of course, there are actual victims. *The use of Victim/Creator here is meant to make sense out of work and reasonably functioning interpersonal relationships.* Certainly in natural disasters, in homicides, in abusive relationships, in educational inequities, etc., and in the injustice that happens on the streets so often, there are people who are indeed victims!

APPENDIX C

The Waterline Model

What is really causing this work disruption?

The following model helps illuminate workplace disruptions differently by using a systemic lens. The Waterline Model enables you to select and solve the right area, so you can avoid continually solving the same problem only to have it resurface.

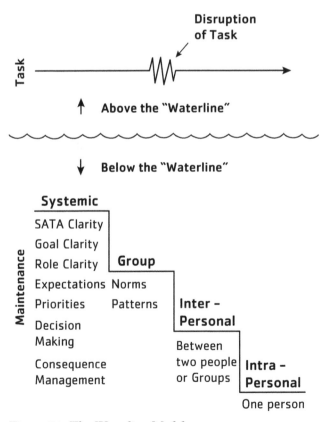

Figure 31 The Waterline Model

The premise is simple. When a task is disrupted, where do you focus to solve the problem? If your organization is like most, then likely you or your employees will blame a person or department. Using systemic principles, the last area to blame is an individual or department. Instead, follow the logic on the next page.

Use Figure 31 to assess your situation and develop a plan to set your workplace on the path of greater alignment and functionality.

The Waterline Model is fairly self-explanatory. *Task* refers to any work task, process, or procedure that must be accomplished daily or periodically for the workplace to succeed. *Maintenance* refers to anything happening below the waterline that would create tension or stop the task from being accomplished.

Most workplaces focus on the wrong place to resolve problems when tasks are disrupted, and then blame individuals or departments.

The first focus area below the waterline is systemic (see Figure 31). Make sure clear foundations are in place for each systemic area that could be contributing to the problem. Then go step by step down the waterline until potentially finding yourself at the last step, intrapersonal. Yes, sometimes the problem really is just a person, yet the likelihood is slim.

I have worked with many organizations where the presenting problem is one group blaming another. After digging deeper and clarifying goals, roles, expectations, and decision making in the troubled areas and helping the correct sponsor to drive, then suddenly the problem disappeared.

Read *Strategic Organizational Alignment* to learn more about the underlying theories described in this appendix. Further, the activities in this book provide models to solve work problems at the *systemic*, *group*, and *interpersonal* levels.

Conclusion

The Waterline Model helps you recognize systemic problems when un-covering moments of tension at work. Ask yourself, "What is below the waterline?" and do not get seduced by the temptation to blame a person as the first resort. Instead think systemic, then group, then interpersonal. Use this model to solve problems at their root, rather than getting stuck in a cycle of quick fixes.

APPENDIX D

Work Team Survey

This appendix contains two assessments: 1) an intact workgroup survey to develop a work team as outlined in Chapter 4 and 2) a survey used to help a merger succeed. The second survey will show how to integrate different surveys based on your scenario.

In addition, when I give the 12 questions during a workgroup, I use weighted scoring. I explain how and what is meant by weighted scoring. Weighted scoring is one of three options I present to score surveys while giving the benefits and drawbacks of each.

The first questionnaire is derived from a 137-question survey delivered to more than 500 companies called the People Performance Profile (PPP). The PPP was created by Robert P Crosby and John Scherer with help from many experts from their respective fields, such as Dr. Ronald Lippitt of the University of Michigan and Dr. Jack Sherwood of Purdue University. The PPP instrument was researched in terms of validity and reliability by Dr. Ron Short and achieved a reliability score of $r = .95$, an astoundingly high score. The validity score was equally as high.

Robert P Crosby's book *Walking the Empowerment Tightrope* outlines 25 factors derived from the PPP in which the top-performing work groups excel. Excel in those factors and you will have high performance in every metric.

The following 12 questions are derived from that work. Therefore, one can infer the validity and reliability of these questions are high.

Work Team Survey

Instructions

Do not sign name.

Answer each question using the following scale.

A (almost always), F (frequently), O (occasionally), S (seldom), N (almost never)

1. Role Clarity. The expectations of my work are clear.
2. Role Clarity. I am asked to do things outside my job duties.
3. Input Needs (materials, information, and equipment). We get, with quality and on time, what we need to do our work.
4. Throughput. We are optimally organized to produce a quality output.
5. Outputs (results of our work). We provide others, with quality and on time, what they need to do their work.
6. Meetings. Our meetings are effective.
7. Meetings. At the end of our meetings, actions are clearly written and include an identified SPA and By-When.
8. Meetings. Actions assigned in prior meetings are reviewed as part of our meeting structure. Individual actions are reviewed in two dimensions: 1) How well were they completed, and 2) are we achieving the intended results?
9. Decision Making. Among the people I interact with, it is clear who decides what and when, who is consulted before key decisions, and who is informed afterward. Plus, we execute effectively.
10. Decision Making. I wait for someone to make a decision about my work before completing the task.
11. Work Data Flow. There is a clear process to resolve work issues (impacting productivity, safety, quality, or cost).
12. Work Data Flow. My supervisor gives feedback about my performance, both positive and negative.

Scoring Surveys

There are many ways to score surveys. Here are three options, with my preference being option 3.

Comparing Scoring Options

Option 1 - Indicate the median (middle) of the respondents' scores.

Question 3. Input Needs (materials, information, and equipment). We get, with quality and on time, what we need to do our work.

	A	F	O	S	N
Respondents' Scores →	0	7	3	0	0

↑ ←—— Median

Option 2 - Calculate the mean using a 1 to 5 linear scale.

Question 3. Input Needs (materials, information, and equipment). We get, with quality and on time, what we need to do our work.

Total Respondents

	A	F	O	S	N	
Respondents' Scores →	0	7	3	0	0	= 10
Linear Scale →	5	4	3	2	1	
Respondents' Scores x Equal Weights →	0	28	9	0	0	= 37

Total of the Respondents' Scores x the Linear Scores

The mean (average) equals the total of the Respondents' Scores x the Linear Scale, divided by the total Respondents. Therefore $37 \div 10 = 3.70$.

Option 3 - Calculate the mean using weighted scoring per answer.

Question 3. Input Needs (materials, information, and equipment). We get, with quality and on time, what we need to do our work.

Total Respondents

	A	F	O	S	N	
Respondents' Scores →	0	7	3	0	0	= 10
Weighted Scores →	5	1	0	0	0	
Respondents' Scores x Weighted Scores →	0	7	0	0	0	= 7

Total of the Respondents' Scores x the Weighted Scores

The mean (average) equals the total of the Respondents' Scores x the Weighted Scores, divided by the total Respondents. Therefore $7 \div 10 = .70$.

Figure 32 Survey Scoring Options

The first option is to indicate the median (mid point) of the respondents' scores, as shown in Figure 32. This option shows the number of respondents for each answer of each question and starts the conversation. It is my least favorite option. However, it is the quickest if you do not have access to quickly calculate the mean.

The second option uses a linear scale, per answer, to calculate the mean for each score. This option allows you to easily calculate the mean. Generation of the mean allows you to compare your scores with other groups and the whole organization. The problem with option two is that it treats each answer as equal when they are not.

Finally, option three weighs each answer regarding its importance to the question to create the mean and comparison scores. This option is by far my favorite because it places appropriate value on each answer.

The three options highlight potential problems differently (see Figure 32). Although I used the same respondents' scores to illustrate the different ways to score the surveys, the mean using linear scoring is 3.70, while the mean using weighted scores is .70. That paints quite a different picture. Weighting the scores is more complicated. Yet, I believe it yields the best results.

Weighted Scoring

Weighted scoring when giving a work team survey creates a more accurate picture of the situation. Why? Because the weighting reflects the importance of each particular answer to each question and highlights issues in a unique way. Take question 3, for example: if you only get the inputs you need to do your job on time occasionally, then that answer is worth zero points. Employees should almost always receive the tools to complete their task. Do you agree? Remember, Gallup found that only "3 in 10 U.S. employees strongly agree they have the materials and equipment they need to do their work right." If you do not weight the scores, then you risk employees not taking the mean as seriously and, therefore, miss issues that could help improve productivity.

To further illustrate, think about this question: "I receive my paycheck on time each month." What weight would you give if the answer was *frequently*? What about *occasionally*?

Weighting can be adjusted to suit your needs or beliefs.

However, only use weighted scoring if you follow up with a process as outlined on page 40. Why? Because weighting the scores paints a clearer picture of problems, and if you do not allow employees to engage to solve those problem, it will likely increase hopelessness in your organization.

The same principle applies to any workplace survey no matter how it is scored. Most employee surveys lower morale and are a missed opportunity to help understand the issues underneath the survey answers. Remember, answers to surveys are not the real issues. Answers just point to issues that must be flushed out by the employees who took the survey. Only the employees know the issues they were thinking about while taking it.

Figure 33 represents the weights I give to the answers of each of the 12 questions on page 132. *When using weighted scores, do not tell the respondents that answers are weighted before they complete the survey, as it can skew the results.*

Weighted Scores By Question

	A	F	O	S	N
Question 1	5	2	0	0	0
Question 2	0	0	1	3	5
Question 3	5	1	0	0	0
Question 4	5	1	0	0	0
Question 5	5	1	0	0	0
Question 6	5	2	0	0	0
Question 7	5	2	0	0	0
Question 8	5	2	0	0	0
Question 9	5	3	1	0	0
Question 10	0	0	1	3	5
Question 11	5	1	0	0	0
Question 12	2	5	2	0	0

Figure 33 Weighted Scores by Question

Work Team Results

1. Role Clarity. The expectations of my work are clear.

A	F	O	S	N
2	7	1	0	0

2. Role Clarity. I am asked to do things outside of my job duties.

A	F	O	S	N
0	2	2	4	2

3. Input Needs (materials, information, and equipment). We get, with quality and on time, what we need to do our work.

A	F	O	S	N
0	7	3	0	0

4. Throughput. We are optimally organized to produce a quality output.

A	F	O	S	N
1	5	4	0	0

5. Outputs (results of our work). We provide others, with quality and on time, what they need to do their work.

A	F	O	S	N
2	6	2	0	0

6. Meetings. Our meetings are effective.

A	F	O	S	N
1	5	3	1	0

7. Meetings. At the end of our meetings, actions are clearly written and include an identified SPA and By-When.

A	F	O	S	N
0	5	4	1	0

8. Meetings. Actions assigned in prior meetings are reviewed as part of our meeting structure. Individual actions are reviewed in two dimensions: 1) how well were they completed, and 2) are we achieving the intended results?

A	F	O	S	N
0	3	4	2	0

9. Decision Making. Between the people that I interact with at work, it is clear who decides what and when, who is consulted before key decisions, and who is informed afterward. Plus, we execute effectively.

A	F	O	S	N
1	6	3	0	0

10. Decision Clarity. I wait for someone to make a decision about my work before completing the task.

A	F	O	S	N
1	2	4	2	1

11. Work Data Flow. When I have a work issue (impacting productivity, safety, quality or costs) there is a clear process to resolve it.

A	F	O	S	N
1	6	1	1	1

12. Work Data Flow. My supervisor gives feedback about my performance, both positive and negative.

A	F	O	S	N
2	5	2	1	0

Figure 34 Survey Results Using Weighted Scores

Figure 34 shows a scored survey using weighted scoring, including the means of all other groups in the organization. The means of other groups help draw comparisons to the immediate workgroup. As you can see in Figure 34, the weighting highlights categories that require improvement. In contrast, if you use linear scoring or indicate only the median of the respondent scores (see Figure 32), then you gain a very different picture than the weighted survey despite using the same respondent scores with the same workgroup. You may achieve the same results without the weighted scoring, but I believe the weighting reveals issues in a much more striking and accurate way. It is a built-in "cheating catcher." In one organization a group agreed to score everything one point higher because they were afraid the results would get them in trouble. Using weighted scoring, it didn't matter. Linear scoring would have disguised their reality.

Their surprised response: "How did you know?" With explanation and good facilitation, the issues surfaced, and the session went quite well!

Remember, using the process in Chapter 4, *the critical data are the issues behind the numbers* that are only known by the actual employees (respondents) in the workgroup. It is dangerous to impose anything on a workgroup because of their scores, especially if it is done many layers above the workgroup. Instead, use surveys as a tool of engagement. The steps in Chapter 4 are repeatable, easy to use, and help employees engage to solve their issues.

Example Merger Survey

Mergers and acquisitions are often implemented in ways that increase stress and the potential of misinformation. High-level leaders, trying to help ease the stress of newly acquired employees, often create expectations that are impossible to deliver, such as "No one will be laid off as a result of this merger" or "You all will receive a raise to match our other locations."

This survey was created while helping a group align goals. They just merged and had concerns about the integration.

Merger Questions

1. The integration between Columbia and Engineered Products is:

Not Working Well   Working Well
  1   2   3   4   5   6   7   8   9   10

2. The (new) centralized areas as a result of the integration (Engineering, Sales, and Customer Service) are:

Not Working Well   Working Well
  1   2   3   4   5   6   7   8   9   10

3. As a result of the integration, I know who to contact for help.

Almost Never   Almost Always
  1   2   3   4   5   6   7   8   9   10

4. Task and decision authority are in the right hands to get my job done (i.e., I rarely have to wait for someone to do or decide something I can do myself).

Always Waiting   The Right Hands
  1   2   3   4   5   6   7   8   9   10

5. It's easy for me and my workgroup to receive needed inputs (materials, information, and equipment) from the intergrated groups and departments providing support.

Almost Never   Almost Always
  1   2   3   4   5   6   7   8   9   10

6. My work team receives enough information about the division integration.

No Information   Enough Information
  1   2   3   4   5   6   7   8   9   10

Figure 35 Merger Survey Example

The survey in Figure 35 was combined with about six questions from the intact work team survey. You can use either scoring system. My aim is to show you how to adapt Chapter 4 to address other workplace concerns.

Conclusion

Survey feedback outlined in Chapter 4 eliminates confusion efficiently and solves many small problems impacting productivity. Also, by using the system-wide cascade process, you engage your entire workplace to directly improve the organization one workgroup dialogue at a time. Dr. Fred Fosmire, former vice president of Organizational and Employee Relations at Weyerhaueser, writes: "Survey feedback methods, when implemented competently by managers who are receptive to feedback, may be the most powerful way we know to improve organization effectiveness." Add weighted scoring and you will highlight the majority of issues within your organization and quickly be on a path to increased productivity.

APPENDIX E

What Is a Goal?

A remarkable number of leaders do not have measurable goals,
which significantly increases the chance of misalignment, in fighting,
and confusion of direction.

In Chapter 2 of *SOA*, I explain how to transform any statement into a goal. This appendix provides examples to help you solidify the concept and develop clear measurable goals. *The lead in leadership is knowing where you are headed.* This appendix will help you with that clarity.

A goal is numeric and measurable. Many people confuse actions, values, standards, statements, beliefs, and other things with goals. Almost all of these items can be transformed into my definition of a goal. Here are examples from various workplaces:

Example 1—Nonprofit Work Process Goal

Belief: High school students increase their chance of graduation if they complete their homework on time.

Action: I will meet weekly with my students to ensure their home work is completed on time.

Goal: My students will complete their assignments by the deadline 90% of the time.

Once the above clarity is achieved, then track the percentage of time the assignments are completed by the deadline and implement actions to address reoccurring issues. Also track the theory—students completing homework have higher graduation rates—to confirm its success by achieving the process goal.

Remember, work process goals represent *the art of managing* and must be managed and adjusted until you track the right processes that lead to the right bottom-line goals. This example goal is about high school graduation.

Example 2—Manufacturing Plant Work Process Goal

Belief: If we increase our speed of changing products on the line, then we will reduce waste and increase machine efficiency.

Action: Set a new standard for product changeovers on the floor.

Standard: Changeover a product in 45 minutes.

Goal: Reach the new product changeover standard 85% of the time. Setting and communicating clear goals and holding the Sustaining Sponsors accountable will improve employee behavior to achieve the goal.

If you follow up such goals with a group process and a problem-solving methodology that involves the people who do the work (Example 2, those responsible for changeovers), then the chances of reaching the new goal are drastically increased.

Conclusion

Setting clear, measurable goals is critical to ensure balance in your workplace and align employees to focus on the right improvements. Review Chapter 2, Goals of SOA for a variety of topics on goals, such as the importance of balance.

APPENDIX F

Conflict Climate Index

All workplaces have conflict. However, not all know how, nor are they ready, to constructively use conflict moments to help improve their workplace. The following conditions can significantly increase your capacity to use conflict toward constructive means. The Conflict-Management Climate Index is derived from the work of Robert P Crosby and John Scherer.

Purpose: To evaluate your organization with regard to its conflict management climate and implement a plan to ensure better outcomes.

Instructions: Rate your organization on the following dimensions. Circle the number that best corresponds to how the organization functions today.

1. Accountability

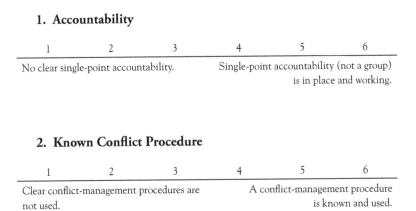

1	2	3	4	5	6
No clear single-point accountability.			Single-point accountability (not a group) is in place and working.		

2. Known Conflict Procedure

1	2	3	4	5	6
Clear conflict-management procedures are not used.			A conflict-management procedure is known and used.		

3. Use of Third Parties

1	2	3	4	5	6

No one uses third parties to help resolve conflicts.

Trained third parties are used frequently to help resolve conflicts.

4. Power of Third Parties

1	2	3	4	5	6

Third parties are usually superiors in the organization.

Third parties are usually people of equal or lower rank.

5. Neutrality of Third Parties

1	2	3	4	5	6

Third parties are never neutral but serve as advocates for a certain outcome.

Third parties are always neutral as to substantive issues.

6. Leadership Conflict Behavior

1	2	3	4	5	6

Leaders do not deal openly with conflicts, but work behind the scenes to resolve them.

Leaders confront conflict directly and work openly with those involved to resolve them.

7. Follow-up

1	2	3	4	5	6

Agreements always fall through the cracks; the same problems must be solved again and again.

Accountability is built into every conflict resolution agreement.

Conflict-Management Climate Index Scoring and Interpretation Sheet

Instructions: To calculate your overall Conflict-Management Climate Index, total the ratings you assigned to the seven separate scales. The highest possible score is 42 and the lowest is 7.

Compare your score with the following conflict resolution-readiness index range.

Index Range Indication

32–42 Ready to work on conflict with little or no work on culture.

17–32 Possible with some commitment to work on culture.

07–16 Very risky without serious work on culture.

Find your lowest ratings and study the following descriptions or interpretations of the separate dimensions. As you read the descriptions, think about what specifically might be done (or changed) in other activities described, to increase your organization's readiness to manage conflict more effectively.

Accountability

Here are the basics of accountability. 1) Is the task or role specifically clear? 2) Is there single point accountability (SPA) of who is responsible? 3) Is there a clear By-When and/or service standard time frame? 4) If the person does not meet their task's time commitments nor communicates effectively to those receiving the task or service, then are appropriate reprimands being consistently applied?

The problem in many organizations is that managers do not apply appropriate reprimands. Consequently, if the basics are in place yet the forth item above is not applied, then there is no consequence for inappropriate behavior and no accountability.

The extremes of managing are laissez faire on one end and autocratic on the other. The more laissez faire or autocratic an organization, the more likely conflicts will arise among employees. A recent study of the prevalence of destructive leadership behavior found that by far the most prevalent type of destructive leadership is laissez faire. Ironically, the least common form was tyrannical leadership, which equates to autocratic leadership. The characteristics of laissez-faire leadership (avoidant, passive, or indirect) create a climate in which accountability is very difficult.

Known Conflict Procedure

Chapters 5 and 6 in Volume I and Chapter 4 in Volume II present step-by-step guides to handle three separate conflict scenarios. For organizations that have clearly defined procedures or channels for conflict resolution, the work of a third-party consultant—whether internal or external to the organization—is obviously much easier. In a system that has no clearly defined ways to resolve conflict and people do not know what to expect or what to do when conflict arises, the work of the third party is extremely difficult.

If people do not think they are safe using a conflict resolution procedure or it appears that the third party is fumbling through it, then they are less likely to have confidence in the outcome. However, even if they do not think they are safe and the third-party facilitator is less than perfect, consistently applied sponsorship through the entire process will still likely yield positive outcomes.

After a conflict procedure is chosen, then leadership alignment from the top and throughout the organization is key to build and drive sponsorship. If top management seriously wants effective conflict management, then the specific procedure must be communicated, expectations must be set, and managers at all levels must be held accountable to ensure they use the procedure with their employees.

Use of Third Parties

A healthy conflict-management climate has trained people to use as third-party facilitators when conflicts arise. Many organizations have, at least tacitly, established the norm that conflict must be kept "in the family" and not "aired in public." Such strategies to work around conflicts miss the point and ensure dysfunction remains.

Strong sponsorship is critical for effective third-party conflict resolution. The boss of each employee must be clear that this is to be done and is not optional (p. 65). Also, the boss must be specific about improvement areas (many conflicts at work are disrupting productivity so each boss needs to know how there participant will resolve specific work problems) resulting from resolution process in addition to what the participants need to work through themselves.

Healthy use of third parties should not be a choice. Clear sponsorship and consistent use of third parties when conflicts disrupt work are key to creating system health.

Power of Third Parties

As Walton (1969) notes, it is difficult for someone with hierarchical power to be an effective third party (see p. 92, Chapter 8). When subordinates believe their comments may later be used against them, then crucial information will likely not be shared during the conflict resolution process. However, this data frequently is a key to unlock conflict situations. In a healthy conflict-management climate, supervisors ensure subordinates seek third-party help from someone on their level or lower in the organization. This approach is difficult for most managers because they want to be helpful and caring and control potentially explosive situations.

Neutrality of Third Parties

Third parties from within the organization must remain neutral about substantive outcomes or at least suppress their biases sufficiently to be effective (see p. 81, Chapter 7). When third parties are unskilled and biased about the conflict resolution outcome, then one party may think they are being "ganged up on." Third-party facilitators that are not trained in how to be neutral may defuse the issue, but are more likely to cause those involved to 1) submerge their real feelings, 2) decrease trust in management, and 3) reduce participant ownership of the resolution that they may think has been imposed on them.

In addition, past experience with a biased third party makes it difficult for members of the organization to trust the process in the future. If that is the case, then the third-party consultant must spend extra time and energy to establish neutrality and credibility with those involved.

Leadership Conflict Behavior

The senior people in any organization greatly influence the climate. Walton and Dutton (1969) showed it is possible to characterize a general style of conflict management in an organization and that the people at the top of the organization set the style by their behavior. In their "contingency theory" of organization, Lawrence and Lorsch (1969) found that not only could they characterize the way people generally approached conflict but also they showed that one particular approach, "confrontation," worked best and was associated with organizational effectiveness. In other words, these researchers/consultants found the way people approach conflict is not a contingency factor, but that there was a "best way" confrontation. It means that conflict is openly recognized when it occurs, and the people involved proceed to deal directly with the conflict. It means *not* running away, *not* trying to "smooth over" real differences, *not* immediately trying to "split the difference," and *not* fighting a win-lose battle. Confrontation implies creative problem solving. Superiors are seen as strong when confronting conflicts, and their behavior encourages others to deal directly with conflict. The model set by those in positions of power has effects on all sorts of subordinate behavior, but especially influences how subordinates relate to each other when dealing with conflicts.

I do not want to downplay how difficult it is to do the above and how much it is contrary to my own findings when working in organizations. In fact, an instrument given to over 1,000 managers indicates that more than 80% either avoid or give in to the other as a primary conflict style. To appropriately confront conflict, managers must learn new skills and develop the discipline to use them even when feeling uncomfortable. Developing a positive conflict climate requires training people to manage conflicts outside of traditional HR practices. Such a structure aids differences to be worked through openly and confidently. For instance, the conflict model presented in Chapter 6 was developed in collaboration with HR and seen as either a HR preventative intervention or, if unsuccessful (rare), a preparation for a traditional HR practice.

Engagement cultures work through conflict. In contrast, the definition of *an actively disengaged employee is one who is not resolving their conflicts.*

Supervisors who use a nonconfrontational style successfully to solve a particular problem weaken the organization's problem-solving and conflict resolution capacity because they reinforce that it is OK, or even preferable, to be indirect. Of course, once in a while indirect resolution is OK. But, if indirect resolution is used as a consistent practice, then dysfunctional systemic norms will be created.

Follow-Up

Chapter 10 of *SOA* is titled Follow-Up. Use it to further develop your ability to follow up and be diligent in following the follow-up strategies for each activity in this book.

Follow-up procedures and methods of accountability should be built into all conflict resolution action plans. It is possible to have a highly successful dialogue between two people, reach intelligent resolutions, and then have the resolutions disappear between the "cracks" in the relationship or the organization's busy work schedule. The last step in the initial conflict resolution process must specify the plan.

1. Who will do what and By-When?
2. Structures are in place to monitor progress.
3. How, when, and by whom will the results of the plan be evaluated?

When the right sponsor(s) ensures that planned outcomes are implemented, the work of a third party is easy. In places where problems historically must be solved over and over again, the third-party consultant must train the sponsors on effective follow-up structure and procedures before addressing the conflict.

Conclusion

The Conflict Climate Index is a quick way to diagnose your workplace and analyze potential strategies to increase the capability for effective conflict utilization. Excellent conflict management does not equate to eventual resolution. Alignment, follow-through, and system health all play a critical part. Use this tool to help you implement the right ingredients to be successful.

APPENDIX G

Emotions at Work

"There is no place for emotions at work."
"Let us remove emotions from this conversation."
"There is no conflict here."

Behavioral Science and the Brain

The above statements directly or indirectly refer to emotionality at work and are, ironically, laden with emotion. Each statement was said to me during my experience inside of organizations. They are attempts to deny that emotion exists or is important in the workplace. While those statements were being made, neuroscientists have been in an intense period of learning about the brain and emotionality. We live in an exciting time for understanding the brain. During the past 25 years, neuroscientists have begun both to unlock its mysteries and reveal some of its underpinnings. Among those understandings is a multitude of ways to keep your brain healthy by, among other things, continuing to develop it throughout your life. Yes, that is right! Throughout!

During my childhood, people thought that your brain and its embedded behavioral patterns fully developed by age five. We now know that this is not true. In fact, the initial development of the brain is completed around the age of 25. But it gets better: the brain keeps developing throughout your life!

We continually either help or hinder our brain development. All learning, no matter how small, creates new neuropathways in your brain. By reading a book, watching educational shows, and learning anything new (golf, language, craft, directions, interpersonal skills, technical skills, etc.), you help your brain. On the flip side, drug or alcohol abuse, abusive relationships, car accidents, bad sleep habits, unhealthy diets, and so on damage your brain.

We also know that emotions truly drive your behavior. In our larger Emotional Intelligence Leadership training, we help people understand and pay attention to their emotions to gain a greater ability to control their behavior, especially in tense moments. Skills are needed during tense moments to slow down and allow your neocortex to help choose your behavior wisely, rather than react in predictable patterns.

Through neuroscience we also know that the limbic region of your brain, which is the seat of your emotions, has 100 neurons headed to your neocortex to each one coming back and that one is one-fourth the size. Your emotions drive your behavior, period. So don't fight it. Instead, try to understand yourself as best you can and learn how to *"feel what you feel yet choose what you do."*

Understanding your brain increases your ability to see, catch, and manage your behavior during difficult moments of your life.

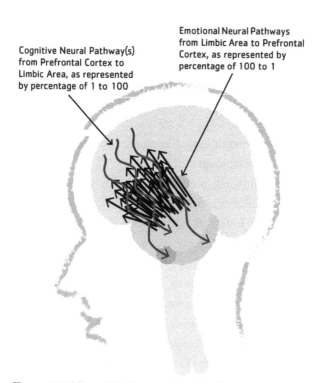

Cognitive Neural Pathway(s) from Prefrontal Cortex to Limbic Area, as represented by percentage of 1 to 100

Emotional Neural Pathways from Limbic Area to Prefrontal Cortex, as represented by percentage of 100 to 1

Figure 36 Neural Pathways from Limbic to Prefrontal Cortex

This appendix provides a scale of emotions at work to help you understand where you are and begin to raise your skills in managing your behavior in difficult moments. It was co-written with Leslie Eastwood.

> "As a graduate student in Leadership and Consulting at the Leadership Institute of Seattle (LIOS), I had the privilege of attending while Robert P Crosby, the founder of LIOS, was still on faculty. His explanation of the impact of emotionality in the workplace struck me as profound. These stages have guided my professional and personal life. What follows is a summary of the explanation of these stages, as presented by Robert P Crosby." (Leslie Eastwood)

Developmentally, we are hard wired as newborns to be fully in touch with our emotions, but through the process of acculturation, humans are parented or schooled to suppress or disconnect from our emotions in certain ways. All too frequently parents, mostly inadvertently yet sometimes consciously, admonish children by saying things such as "Stop crying," or "You shouldn't feel upset about that," and the rest of Western society follows suit with expectations that emotional displays are unacceptable and should be avoided. However, emotions are real, with accompanying physical attributes, often leaving powerful imprints on memories that may change our perceptions of events.

Figure 37 shows a continuum of individual awareness of how emotions impact the workplace from the least aware and narrowest array of responses to the most aware and widest array of responses.

Awareness of Emotions at Work

Level	Description
5	Embraces the unfolding of awareness that the self and others co-create their mutual experiences. —the response is "we do this dance together."
4	Recognizes one's unique history contributes to their own emotional impact. —the response is "aha, I push my own buttons."
3	Emotions impact the workplace, yet the focus is external on the other person. —the response is blame "you push my buttons."
2	Emotions are a factor in the workplace, but are a nuisance or distraction. —the response is discomfort or avoidance.
1	Emotions have no place at work and should have no impact on behavior. —the response is denial or pretense.

Figure 37 Awareness of Emotions at Work

The chart is intended to help you reflect on your own awareness or reactivity around emotions at work and provide a path forward. Awareness and acknowledgment of the stages is a good place to start a journey of discovery. Functioning at level five requires tremendous work.

Where would you rate your level of awareness of emotions?

We believe that once level five is achieved, then how we impact each other at work, home, in our communities, and across the planet significantly improves. Gaining full maturity and awareness of the power of emotions to inform our choices opens a wide range of options from which to navigate life.

Conclusion

Emotions simply exist. They play an important role in driving behavior. In fact, modern neuroscience makes a strong case that your emotions drive your behavior more than anything else. To the extent that it is true, the only logical thing to do is to try and honor and understand our emotions to behave as rationally as possible. Once you lose the fear of emotions, then you will thrive in your workplace, easily work through difficult moments, and create a more productive environment. If you operate at Level 1 or Level 2, then that prospect becomes more challenging. Yet, training and working on emotional intelligence can begin to reverse the trend and move the system toward health.

Bibliography

Aasland, M. S., A. Skogstad, G. Notelaers, M. B. Nielsen, and S. Einarsen. 2010. "The Prevalence of Destructive Leadership Behaviour." *British Journal of Management* 21, pp. 438–52.

Bowen, M., and M. E. Kerr. 1988. *Family Evaluation.* New York, NY: W.W. Norton & Company.

Crosby, C. P. 2017. *Strategic Organizational Alignment.* New York, NY: Business Expert Press, LLC.

Crosby, G. L. 2015. *Fight, Flight, Freeze.* Seattle, WA: CrosbyOD Publishing.

Crosby, G. L. 2017. *Leadership Can Be Learned.* New York, NY: CRC Press, Taylor & Francis Group, Productivity Press.

Crosby, R. P. 2011. *Culture Change in Organizations.* Seattle, WA: CrosbyOD Publishing.

Crosby, R. P. 2015. *The Cross-Functional Workplace.* Seattle, WA: CrosbyOD Publishing.

Crosby, R. P. 2006. *Get Unstuck from Fundamentalism.* Seattle, WA: Vivo Publishing Co., Inc.

Crosby, R. P., and J. Scherer. 1981. *Diagnosing Organizational Conflict-Management Climates.* La Jolla, CA: University Associates Publishers.

Crosby, R. P., and Scherer, J. 1989. *People Performance Profile.* Narberth, PA: Computer Profiles, Inc.

Crosby, R. P. 1992. *Walking the Empowerment Tightrope.* King of Prussia, PA: Organization Design and Development, Inc.

Friedman, E. 1985. *Generation to Generation.* New York, NY: Guilford Press.

Gallup Inc. 2017. *State of the American Workplace.* Washington, D.C.

Hall, J. 1969. *Conflict Management Survey.* Teleometrics International Inc.

Lewin, K. May, 1939. "Patterns of Aggressive Behavior in Experimentally Created Social Climates." *Journal of Social Psychology* 10, no. 2, pp. 271–99.

Lewin, K. 1997. *Resolving Social Conflicts & Field Theory in Social Science.* Washington, D.C.: American Psychological Associates.

Lippitt, G., and R. Lippitt. 1986. *The Consulting Process in Action,* 2nd ed. San Diego, CA: University Associates.

Merrill, D. W., and R. H. Reid. 1981. *Personal Style and Effective Performance.* Radner, PA: Chilton.

Minuchin, S. 1974. *Families and Family Therapy.* Cambridge, MA: Harvard University Press.

Rogers, C. 1951. *Client-Centered Therapy.* Boston, MA: Houghton Mifflin.

Schmuck, R. A., S. E. Bell, and W. E. Bell. 2012. *The Handbook of Organization Development in Schools and Colleges.* Santa Cruz, CA: Exchange Point International.

Walton, R. E. 1987. *Managing Conflict.* Reading, MA: Addison-Wesley Publishing Company, Inc.

Weisbord, M. R. 2012. *Productive Workplaces.* San Francisco, CA: Jossay-Bass.

Whitaker, C. A., and W. M. Bumberry. 1988. *Dancing with the Family.* New York, NY: Brunner/Mazel Publishers.

Whitaker, C. A., and A. Y. Napier. 1978. *The Family Crucible.* New York, NY: Harper & Row.

Williamson, D. 1991. *The Intimacy Paradox.* New York, NY: Guilford Press.

About the Author

Chris Crosby began his organization development career in 1993. He combines a business-results focus with applied behavior science and group process to help engage your employees to achieve greater results. His work spans public, private, and nonprofit industries across five continents. He is an expert in designing small and large experiential activities to solve various challenges, including mergers, large cross-functional projects, and whole-system transformations.

Chapter Index

APPENDIX INDEX

OTHER TITLES IN THE STRATEGIC MANAGEMENT COLLECTION

John A. Pearce II, Villanova University, *Editor*

- *First and Fast: Outpace Your Competitors, Lead Your Markets, and Accelerate Growth* by Stuart Cross
- *Strategies for University Management* by J. Mark Munoz and Neal King
- *Strategies for University Management, Volume II* by J. Mark Munoz and Neal King
- *Strategic Organizational Alignment: Authority, Power, Results* by Chris Crosby
- *Business Strategy in the Artificial Intelligence Economy* by J. Mark Munoz and Al Naqvi

Announcing the Business Expert Press Digital Library

Concise e-books business students need for classroom and research

This book can also be purchased in an e-book collection by your library as

- a one-time purchase,
- that is owned forever,
- allows for simultaneous readers,
- has no restrictions on printing, and
- can be downloaded as PDFs from within the library community.

Our digital library collections are a great solution to beat the rising cost of textbooks. E-books can be loaded into their course management systems or onto students' e-book readers.

The **Business Expert Press** digital libraries are very affordable, with no obligation to buy in future years. For more information, please visit **www.businessexpertpress.com/librarians**. To set up a trial in the United States, please email **sales@businessexpertpress.com**.